River~Walking Songbirds & Singing Coyotes

River~Walking Songbirds & Singing Coyotes

An Uncommon Field Guide
to Northwest Mountains

Patricia K. Lichen

Illustrated by Linda M. Feltner

SASQUATCH BOOKS
SEATTLE

Printed in Canada
Distributed in Canada by Raincoast Books, Ltd.
07 06 05 04 03 02 01   6 5 4 3 2 1

Cover and interior design and composition: Kate Basart
Copy editor: Alice Copp Smith

Library of Congress Cataloging in Publication Data
River-walking songbirds and singing coyotes : an uncommon field guide to Northwest mountains / by Patricia Lichen ; illustrations by Linda Feltner.
       p.   cm.
       references; index.
       1. Natural history—Northwest, Pacific. 2. Mountain animals—Northwest, Pacific—Identification. 3. Mountain plants—Northwest, Pacific—Identification. I. Title
QH104.5.N6 L53 2001
508.795—dc21   00-052261

Sasquatch Books
615 Second Avenue
Seattle, Washington 98104
(206) 467-4300
www.SasquatchBooks.com
books@SasquatchBooks.com

For my husband, Tim,
whom I met because Mount St. Helens erupted.

Contents

Acknowledgments

I am grateful to the following experts, each of whom graciously reviewed at least one (and more often several) of these essays: Ric Balfour of the Oregon Forest Resources Institute; Todd Cullings; Peter Frenzen of the Mount St. Helens National Volcanic Monument; Sarah Gage of the University of Washington Herbarium; Esther Howard; Lysbeth Hol; Marilynne Keyser; Tom Pierson of the U.S. Geological Survey; Susan Piper; Robert Michael Pyle; Gail Roberts; Todd R. Seamons; Sarah Smith; Shelley Weisberg of the North Cascades Institute; Adam Winters; and Matt Zaffino, KGW-TV chief meteorologist. Also, Steve Kucas of the Portland Water Bureau supplied information about steelhead. These experts pointed out errors and misinterpretations wherever they occurred. Any inaccuracies that remain in the text are mine alone.

My thanks also to these friends and family members, who have shared with me encounters with the natural world and then allowed me to tell those stories: Celese Brune; Esther Howard; my mother, Mae Rue Hutchison, and my sister, Ann Kirkendall; my daughter, Hallie, and my husband, Tim Lichen; Ralph Naess; Carole Wendler; and Dan White.

I am also indebted to my father, Frederick J. Hutchison, and the members of two writers' groups, Sirius Writers and Chrysalis, who critiqued and improved many of these essays. Special thanks to the stalwart Susan McElheran who, in belonging to both groups, critiqued more of these essays than anyone short of my editor. Among the Sirius Writers, I especially thank Bonnie and Gale Long, Jim Manuel, Dwight Ball Morrill, Tawny Schlieski, and Cord "Bud" Sengstake. Among the Chrysalis group at Clackamas Community College, Oregon City, Oregon, I especially thank Beth Miles, who critiqued many essays outside of the meetings, and our peerless leader, Kate Gray. I am also grateful to the members of both groups for their kind encouragement and enthusiasm for this project.

Introduction

"The birds I heard today, which fortunately, did not come within the scope of my science, sang as freshly as if it had been the first morning of creation." I've always loved this quote by Henry David Thoreau, which reminds me that I don't need to know the name of a songbird (or a fern or a mushroom or a hawk, for that matter) to enjoy it.

Yet, as Thoreau certainly knew, there is joy in being able to recognize a plant or creature wherever we find it, and to greet it by name. As with our other friendships, the more we learn about a particular being's life, the greater our appreciation can grow.

This is the purpose of the *Uncommon Field Guide* series: to enhance our connection to other beings in the natural world, and hopefully to deepen that connection. Each of the three books (*Passionate Slugs & Hollywood Frogs: An Uncommon Field Guide to Northwest Backyards*; *Brittle Stars & Mudbugs: An Uncommon Field Guide to Northwest Shorelines & Wetlands*; and *River-Walking Songbirds & Singing Coyotes: An Uncommon Field Guide to Northwest Mountains*) offers an opportunity to become better acquainted with plants, animals, and phenomena (such as rainbows or lightning) found in the Pacific Northwest.

In each book I've focused on easily recognizable species and phenomena, and those common to a particular Pacific Northwest geographic area. Of course, some of the subjects do not neatly segregate themselves into specific territories, and for that reason their placement has been arbitrary. (For example, the crow, coyote, and horsetails might have ended up in any one of the three books—but the crows landed in the backyard book, coyote found a home in the mountain book, and horsetails sprouted in the shorelines and wetlands book.)

Similarly, some of the creatures and plants within this *Northwest Mountains* book don't restrict themselves to a particular elevation. Still, the subjects have been arranged so that you encounter them in the text just as you might find them on a hike that gains elevation (that is, those found at lower elevations are toward the front of the book, those that prefer higher elevation are situated near the end of the book).

With apologies to those of you living in the eastern part of Washington and Oregon, the essays in all three books focus to a greater degree on the region west of the Cascade Mountains. Please note I often use the shortcut of "Pacific Northwest region" instead of the more accurate (but too cumbersome) phrase "Pacific Northwest region west of the Cascades."

For many years I had the pleasure of working as a naturalist in Washington and Oregon, discussing with people the plants, animals, and natural events of the Northwest as we walked through woods and beside waterfalls, down into caves and along lakeshores. It's my hope that the *Uncommon Field Guide* series continues that work, acting in the capacity of a friendly naturalist who answers your questions, mentions interesting tidbits you might not think to ask, and helps to further both your understanding and your relationship with the natural world.

Oregon Grape

Latin name: *Berberis nervosa* (or *Mahonia nervosa*)

Description: To about 18 inches high; yellow flowers in erect clusters; bluish-purple grapelike fruit; 11 to 21 shiny, hollylike leaflets.

Habitat: Coniferous forests; generally at low to mid-elevations.

Although the name "Oregon grape" has a flavorful ring to it, you shouldn't take it literally: this plant doesn't confine itself to Oregon and its "grapes" are really berries. Even Oregon grape's scientific name carries a cloud of doubt—some taxonomists place it in the genus *Berberis* and others in *Mahonia*.

But there's no argument that Oregon grape is one of the Pacific Northwest's most common forest plants, or that it makes a fine low shrub/groundcover for landscaping. One of my husband's first acts after we'd bought our house was to pull out the pansies along the walkway to the front door and replace them with more dramatic—and native—plants, including an Oregon grape. The plant displays its shiny, green leaflets throughout the year, a few of which occasionally blush red in late summer or fall. In early spring the Oregon grape greets visitors to our door with fragrant clusters of bright yellow flowers, which are replaced, later in the year, with bluish-purple berries.

Those "grapes" are tart but edible; people have been making them into jelly since the days of the settlers. Some Native tribes ate the berries themselves, but others refused to. Many tribes boiled the roots to obtain a yellow pigment used to dye beargrass and other material for basket-making. The boiled roots were also used medicinally to treat coughs, stomach upset, or venereal disease. Today, herbalists still laud Oregon grape, suggesting its various alkaloids, especially berberine, help fight infections and strengthen the immune system. It's also recommended for lowering blood pressure, improving digestion, and stimulating the appetite.

The Pacific Northwest's most common Oregon grape, *Berberis nervosa*, is found in shady forests from low to mid-elevations and is sometimes called long-leaved, mountain, or dull Oregon grape to differentiate it from two other closely related species. Tall Oregon grape (*B. aquifolium*), as its name suggests, can be recognized by its height of two to ten feet. It also usually has between five to nine leaflets compared to *B. nervosa*'s eleven to twenty-one. This species is Oregon's state flower, and it prefers open places such as road edges and clearings. Creeping Oregon grape (*B. repens*), at six to thirty inches high, is also well-described by its common name. This species, with five to seven leaflets, is found on the east side of the Cascades.

The distinctive leaflets on all three of these plants earned them the name "Oregon holly." The prickly-looking greenery easily distinguishes each of these species from any other shrub in the Northwest, whether it is found growing on the moist forest floor, clambering up a dry, open slope, or enlivening the walkway to someone's front door.

Porcupine

Latin name: *Erethizon dorsatum*

Description: About 28 to 36 inches long, including tail; stout body covered with black fur; long yellowish guard hairs partially obscure quills when they are not erect.

Habitat: Young and old forests, especially open ones; woody vegetation along streams and marshy areas.

A porcupine is one of those animals you don't mistake for anything else. When one stepped out of the forest and waddled across the road in front of my truck, I knew what I was looking at. Despite the long yellowish hairs hiding most of its quills, there was no doubt who that ponderous and pigeon-toed creature was.

The porcupine's thirty thousand quills are unlikely to do you any harm as long as you keep a respectful distance. A porcupine is a peaceable creature who typically attempts to flee attack. But if it is unable to reach the safety of a tree or crevice, the porcupine signals its intentions. Keeping its back to the intruder, the animal lowers its head to protect its unarmed muzzle and soft belly, and abruptly raises its hair. The sharp quills are revealed, obvious and ominous. An unschooled harasser who attacks it learns a painful lesson. The porcupine's rear feet stamp about and the tail thrashes, embedding needle-sharp spines as they make contact with boot, leg, snout, or paws. Contrary to folklore, a porcupine cannot "throw" its quills, but they are so loosely connected to the animal's skin that some may be flung off by furious swings of the tail. The heat and moisture of the victim's flesh expand the several dozen tiny barbs on the quills, and, with the victim's every unavoidable muscle twitch, these barbs drive the spines in deeper.

Long after the porcupine has made its escape, its quills continue drilling through the victim's tissue, sometimes working their painful way out the other side. But if a quill should pierce a vital organ, or if so many are embedded in the snout that the animal cannot feed itself, it will die. The porcupine, meanwhile, regrows its barbs in anticipation of the next blundering, uneducated animal it may meet.

Despite its formidable defense, the porcupine is prey to certain animals, including mountain lions and coyotes. But its greatest enemy is the fisher, an animal related to the weasel, which actively hunts porcupines. Although it was once believed that a fisher deftly slipped a paw under a porcupine and flipped it on its back to reach the unprotected belly, it's now known that the porcupine becomes incapacitated after repeated lunges at its vulnerable face.

A staunch vegetarian, a porcupine attacks only trees—to the consternation of foresters. It especially likes conifer needles, growing buds, and the inner cambium layer under the bark. These favored foods make it more likely that you'll find a porcupine high up in a tree than down on the ground. But it also eats grasses, roots, berries, fruits, catkins and other seeds, and wetland plants. When it swims to reach pond-lilies to munch on, the animal's hollow spines add buoyancy. As many cabin-owners and backpackers have learned, porcupines also chew on wood, leather, nylon, and rubber (including tires and other car parts). The most likely explanation for this is that they crave salt, but these food choices may also reflect a need to hone their continuously growing teeth.

The porcupine is a solitary creature without much of a family life. During the fall mating season, males sometimes engage in screaming, biting fights over a female. They occasionally stick one another with their quills (which are later dexterously pulled out with front teeth and forepaws). Once the battle is decided, the victor and his intended may stand up on their hind legs and touch noses during courtship. Then comes the tricky part.

An old joke goes: "How do porcupines make love?" The punchline—"Verrrry carefully"—is not far wrong. They mate in the manner of most mammals, with the male behind the female—after she has conveniently lifted her tail over her back. This allows the male to rest a steadying paw or lean against a nonbristly surface.

Seven months later, the female is ready to birth a single baby, or rarely two. This raises the second prickly how-do-they-do-that question. The baby, endearingly called a porcupette, is covered by a fetal membrane—and its quills are soft. They dry and harden shortly after birth. The porcupette stays with mother for its first six months. Sometime in the fall, ready to live on its own, it waddles off, fully prepared to teach other young animals about the proper respect due a porcupine.

Swallowtail Butterflies

Latin names: *Papilio zelicaon* (anise swallowtail); *P. rutulus*
(western tiger swallowtail); *P. eurymedon* (pale or white tiger swallowtail)

Description: Up to 3⅞ inches wide from wingtip to wingtip, depending
on species. The tiger species have bright yellow to nearly white wings with black
"tiger" stripes that run from the leading edge of the wings toward the body; the anise
are also yellow and black but lack the distinctive stripes. Hind (lower)
wings have trailing lobe and blue and orange spots.

Habitat: Fields, meadows, parks, streamsides, roadsides,
hilltops, mountains, woods, clearings, gardens.

During their brief lifetimes, swallowtails, like most butterflies, basically do three things: bask in the sun, sip sugary nectar, and have sex. Since they spend only one or two weeks in their adult form, it seems fitting that they should live it up.

Of course, before she dies, a female must also lay eggs that contain the next generation of swallowtails. She diligently deposits a few hundred minute eggs, each laid singly, on the undersides of leaves. Upon hatching, a caterpillar generally first eats the remains of its egg and then turns its tiny mandibles toward the leaf it finds itself on. The Northwest's most common swallowtails are the anise, the western tiger, and the pale or white tiger, and each species has particular food plants it favors as a larvae and others it favors as an adult. The western tiger swallowtail, for example, sips nectar from flowers like honeysuckle and sunflowers, but its green larva typically munches high in the tops of willow, alder, or poplar trees. In between feeding bouts, it uses silk from a spinneret near its mouth to roll a protecting leaf around its body.

All swallowtail larvae carry a concealed weapon they reveal when disturbed or attacked: the *osmeterium,* a scent gland located just behind the caterpillar's head. When agitated, the larva rears back its head and abruptly extends this Y-shaped yellow organ. As if that wouldn't be startling enough, the osmeterium also releases an acrid odor. Since this defense is unique to swallowtail larvae—and since the odor is not necessarily offensive to human noses—a gentle poke to any suspected swallowtail caterpillar will quickly confirm (or deny) its identity.

The larvae grow quickly, but since their skin does not, they molt five or more times. For the final molt, the caterpillar attaches itself to a twig. It makes a small silken pad with its spinneret, attaches the tiny hooks of its tail end to it, and then spins a silk thread, called a girdle, around its body and the twig. The girdle acts something like the sling of a telephone-line worker to secure the insect while it undergoes its final, amazing transformation. The last larval skin splits down the back and, with much wiggling and flexing, is shed to reveal a chrysalis, or pupa.

Although the insect now appears to be dormant, enormous changes are happening within the chrysalis. In what would seem a rather intense puberty, tissues and organs are dissolved or reorganized into the adult form. Eight to ten days later, the chrysalis splits and a swallowtail butterfly pulls itself free.

After expanding and drying its wings, the butterfly is ready to take up an adult's pursuit of nectar and sex. To find members of the opposite gender, all an anise or pale swallowtail needs to do is fly to the nearest hill it sees. Other swallowtails, also drawn to the heights, will congregate there. This activity, known by the descriptive and delightful name "hilltopping," is shared by many other butterfly species. However, one of the Northwest's most common butterflies, the western tiger swallowtail, prefers trees that border rivers (or occasionally streets).

The males patrol the area, seeking females of their own species. When a female seductively flutters by, the male pursues her. The butterflies mate by pressing the tips of their abdomens together as he transfers a packet of sperm called a spermatophore to her. When she is ready to lay her eggs, she flies slowly over a likely area, seeking an appropriate food plant for her species. Landing on a plant to investigate it, she confirms its identity with hairlike taste organs on the tips of her forelegs. As she lays her eggs, small amounts of sperm are released from the spermatophore to fertilize them. After depositing one hundred and fifty or more single eggs, she lives only a short time. Like most butterflies, a swallowtail lives fast, dies within a month after emerging from the chrysalis, and leaves a good-looking corpse.

Millipede

Latin name: *Harpaphe haydeniana*

Description: To 3 inches long; dark, cylindrical body with many segments; most segments have two legs on each side; series of bright yellow or orange spots on sides near legs; younger millipedes lighter in color than adults.

Habitat: Forest floors, under stones or logs, in leaf litter, crossing trails.

There seems to be no consensus on what to call our most common millipede, but the best name I've found so far is "night train." After all, the millipede is shaped something like a miniature Amtrak passenger compartment. And its smooth locomotion, dark coloration, and yellow spots are reminiscent of a train with brightly lit windows traveling at night.

But if you're not on board with that name, you might prefer "yellow-spotted" or "almond-scented" millipede. When the millipede is agitated, a pore on each of its segments, advertised by the yellow spots, exudes a minute amount of cyanide. The only effect this has on curious humans is that it registers as a pleasant almond scent, but the substance is strong enough to deter or even kill potential insect predators.

Some species of beetles are able to eat millipedes despite their chemical protection, and larger predators like birds, lizards, and frogs are also unimpressed. The millipede reacts to their onslaughts by coiling up to protect its soft underbelly. You're likely to see this response (and receive a whiff of almonds) if you pick up a night train.

When it's not being pestered by predators or people, the millipede spends its time eating leaf litter and dead plants. This little vegetarian plays an important role in recycling the forest's nutrients, munching decaying leaves despite the tannin that makes them inedible to many species. The nutrients then become available through the animal's waste products.

Like all arthropods, the millipede wears its skeleton on the outside. Though this exoskeleton protects the animal, it also limits growth, so until they reach full size, millipedes regularly molt. Because it is extremely vulnerable while it undergoes this process, the young millipede digs a chamber in the soil and seals itself in for several weeks. While it is entombed, its hard old exterior splits down the back and the millipede pulls free. It will have gained additional segments and legs and is likely to be a shade darker than before. Once the new exoskeleton hardens, the creature can safely excavate itself.

After seven molts over the course of two years, the millipede is full grown. It now has twenty segments, and each of the segments equipped for walking has two pairs of legs. Females have thirty-one pairs of legs, while

males have thirty. The difference occurs at the seventh segment, where one pair of the male's legs have been modified to enable them to transfer sperm from the third body segment, where it is produced. Prior to mating, the male millipede bends its body so that its third and seventh segments are in contact.

Once the sperm, neatly tucked inside a package called a spermatophore, is transferred, the millipede is ready to woo a female. He does so by drumming his many legs upon her back in what must be an enticing rhythm. The two turn belly to belly, press their seventh segments together, and the female receives the spermatophore. She will soon dig a hole in which to lay several hundred eggs.

The baby millipedes that hatch from the eggs are tiny, pale imitations of their parents and have only a few pairs of legs. Nevertheless, the young millipedes shoulder their important job as nutrient recyclers, following in their parents' (many) footsteps.

Trillium

Latin name: *Trillium ovatum*

Description: To 16 inches tall; 3 white flower petals up to 3 inches long; 3 wide oval leaves to 7 inches long; slender stalk. Blooms March through May.

Habitat: Moist woods and streamsides at low to middle elevations.

Trillium is so well known that it could be considered the robin of wildflowers. The creamy white-petaled plant is also one of our best loved wildflowers, perhaps because it is the first one many rain-weary Northwesterners see when they finally venture out into the woods again. Skunk cabbage's February appearance hints at spring, but trillium's March arrival delivers it.

For years, trillium suffered from being *too* well loved. People dazzled by the return of sunshine trooped through the woods, mercilessly plucking the harbingers of spring. But the widely believed notion that trillium won't bloom again for seven years if its flower is picked has probably saved a lot of flowers. Although it's not strictly true, the folklore has its basis in fact. A plant's green leaves manufacture food from sunshine, and trillium—like other perennials—stores that food in its underground rootstock, enabling the plant to bloom again the following year. Because trillium's leaves grow close beneath the flower, rather than at the base of the plant, pickers invariably take the leaves along with the flower. Without leaves, the plant is unable to make food, and it is weakened. The following year it will have to send up a smaller shoot, which will not be able to produce as much food and probably won't be able to flower. It might not really take seven years for a trillium to regain enough energy to flower again, but picking the flower certainly does damage the plant.

And, of course, a picked trillium can't create the seeds that make new plants. Those flowers that escape human predation gradually turn from white to pink to deep rose. Eventually the fertilized flowers wither, die, and are replaced by an oval, three-sided capsule. Numerous seeds are stored inside, each of which has a fleshy little oil-rich appendage called an *elaiosome.*

Although squirrels, chipmunks, and other small animals have been reported to eat trillium seeds, it appears that insects disperse the most seeds. Ants and yellow jackets, attracted to the oil in the elaiosomes, carry the seeds home to their respective clans. After the insects or their larvae consume the elaiosomes, the seeds themselves, apparently unpalatable, are discarded. In effect, trillium manufactures oil to fuel moving-van insects that haul away its next generation, enabling its offspring to set up house elsewhere.

Not everyone calls this plant "trillium." Another common name for it is wake-robin. It's been said by a more poetic writer that the plant's appearance in early spring wakes the robin into song. Those of us who prefer "trillium" are using Latin. Trillium is one of the few plants whose common name is the same as its scientific genus name. The "tri" in the Latin name refers to parts in threes: trillium has three petals, three leaves, and three sepals (the small green modified leaves tucked between neighboring white petals); and its reproductive parts include a three-chambered pistil (female organ) and six pollen-covered stamens (male organs).

The many different Indian tribes in the Northwest were well acquainted with trillium and used it in several ways. Juice from the bulb was used as an eye medicine, and various parts of trillium were employed to treat excessive menstrual bleeding, bronchial problems, diarrhea, and other complaints. Some tribes used the bulb as a love charm, either by pounding it and then rubbing it over the body or by cooking and adding it to the food of a desired lover.

It's easy to see how the first true plant of spring would become a charm for fresh, young love. These days, however, trillium is better known as a very welcome sign of spring. So, during the early days of sunshine, take those you love—or just your own sweet self—for a walk in the woods to be greeted by trillium's simple beauty.

Sword fern

Latin name: *Polystichum munitum*

Description: Fronds 3 to 5 feet long grow from a central point;
each individual leaflet on the frond has a little "thumb" sticking
up near where it attaches to the stem.

Habitat: Moist forests; cool, shady areas of drier forests.

One of my favorite places is an old-growth forest where the strapping cedars and hemlocks stand tall, and below them sword ferns arc in graceful green fountains out of the duff. Although the sword fern adds a certain touch to an ancient forest, it's not particular about the age of its neighbors. Sword fern is a common plant in the Pacific Northwest, abundant in virtually any moist forest west of the Cascades.

Large and obvious, this plant is one of our easiest ferns to recognize. An individual plant's fronds grow outward from the base, like water sprayed from the nozzle of an upturned garden hose. Each spring, fresh green fronds arise from the middle of the plant. These are called fiddleheads because they resemble the scroll at the top of a violin. As they uncoil, their horizontal leaves also spread wide, as if the frond were lifting its head and opening its many arms.

Although I'm not aware of traditional use of these fiddleheads as food, some tribal groups did eat the fern's roots after baking or boiling them. And the Cowlitz and Quileute Indians once gathered sword-fern fronds to use as bedding. Today, sword-fern leaves are collected for background greenery in commercial floral arrangements.

In contrast to plants that flaunt gaudy flowers as a reproductive come-on, sword ferns lead quiet, rather strait-laced sex lives. They reproduce with decorum, forgoing both flowers and seeds. Ferns make more ferns in a two-step process. A mature plant produces small rusty circles, called *sori*, on the underside of its fronds. These circles, which neatly line up along the margins of each leaflet, contain microscopic spores, and each plant produces millions. The spores eventually fall to the ground around the fern or are carried a few feet by the wind. If moisture and light conditions are right, the spores will grow into tiny heart-shaped plants called *prothallia*. It is these that reproduce sexually to become young fern plants. Sperm and egg cells grow on the undersides of prothallia leaves and require a drop of moisture to unite. Then the sperm cells, drawn by a chemical attractant, swim through the water to fertilize the eggs. A fertilized egg divides and redivides and finally creates new leaves unlike those of the heart-shaped prothallium. Additional leaves become more fernlike, eventually taking on the characteristic broad-sword shape for which the sword fern was named.

This two-step system of reproduction developed millions of years ago, before pollinating insects existed. Ferns, one of our planet's oldest known plants, were thriving long before dinosaurs appeared on earth. As I walk among sword ferns during the warmer months, I like to note the progression of this ancient cycle by occasionally tipping up the underside of a frond to see how the sori are developing. Happily, there are many places where I can indulge this habit, in addition to my favorite old-growth forest. Like many Northwesterners, I like to spend time in places where sword ferns still outnumber people.

sori

Douglas-fir

Latin name: *Pseudotsuga menziesii*

Description: To over 250 feet; tall, straight tree; blunt-ended needles borne singly rather than in clusters, with two white stripes on their undersides; cones hang down from branch and have three-pronged, papery bracts tucked under scales.

Habitat: Moist, well-drained soil.

When I drove my parents from the airport on their first visit to the Pacific Northwest, they were impressed by the long unbroken ribbon of evergreens that stretched beside the road. "All the trees here are Christmas trees!" my Midwestern mother exclaimed— and she wasn't far wrong.

The trees we were seeing through the car windows were Douglas-firs, legions of which are shipped East every year for use as Christmas trees. This species not only furnishes a home's holiday cheer, it likely also supplied the lumber for that house, the wood on the sled under the tree, and the wrapping paper that covers the sled. Douglas-fir produces remarkable wood that can be sawn into poles and beams, cut into lumber, peeled into veneer, or pulverized into paper. It is the leading timber tree in North America and one of the most important timber trees in the world.

Douglas-fir has several traits that endear it to those in the lumber business. It's easy to cultivate, grows straight and fast, and produces wood that is both strong and durable. Private tree farms and state and national forests now supply the nation's wood, cutting and replanting in regular rotations, but at one time the Pacific Northwest was so populated with natural stands of these trees that they seemed limitless. Douglas-fir grows elsewhere in the Western states, but it grows nowhere as well as it does in the Northwest. It is by far the most common tree in this region, and if you know how to identify it, you can recognize probably eight out of ten trees in the forest.

The bark of an old, venerable Doug-fir is reddish brown, cracked with deep furrows; younger bark is gray, with blisters of resin. Single needles usually grow all the way around the branches, but if the branches are shaded, they may look as if a comb-wielding mother has tried to part them down the middle. The tiny stomata (openings that exchange gases and let the tree breathe) are located in two white bands on the underside of each needle. Crush a needle between your fingers and you'll smell lemon.

Doug-fir cones are distinctive. Tucked under the scales are three-pronged paper-thin bracts (modified leaves) that have been described as looking like pitchforks or like the tails and hind legs of mice escaping rain or fire. These bracts can also be seen in the bristly female flowers that appear each year at the ends of the twigs. The small, brown male flowers are pointed and covered with scales; they grow on the undersides of the branches. After the male flowers release their pollen, the fertilized female flowers develop into cones that hang down from the branches. Inside each scale are two small seeds, each with a wing. When these are fully developed, they are released by the cone.

The wings can carry the seeds into far-off areas opened by forest fire or winds, where the young Doug-firs thrive. The seedlings are relatively shade intolerant and cannot grow in dark ancient forests. Thus, the Pacific Northwest's most successful tree is not a dominant member of its climax forests; if a forest is left alone, western hemlock and red-cedar will eventually replace Doug-fir.

(This shouldn't imply that the forests seen by the first white explorers were composed solely of hemlock and cedar. Old-growth forests are never static; old trees die and are replaced, and fire traditionally opened vast areas.)

Doug-fir is named after David Douglas, the roaming naturalist who first sent its seeds to England in 1825. It's a lovely coincidence that the Scottish botanist had a last name that can serve as a first. This allows us to refer to our most familiar, useful, and economically important tree by a friendly name, even a nickname: Douglas-fir, Doug-fir.

Banana Slug

Latin name: *Ariolimax columbianus*

Description: 8 to 10 inches long; color ranges from bright yellow through olive green to nearly all black; lighter-colored slugs often have dark splotches.

Habitat: Moist forests; less frequently, in cultivated gardens.

Covered with slime and awfully darn big for a slug, the banana slug may not be one of the Pacific Northwest's more endearing animals—but it is a native. Unlike voracious imported European slugs, banana slugs are found more often in moist woods than in an urban garden.

The next time you see a banana slug, take a close look. You'll notice a hole on its right side, just behind the smooth mantle that covers the front of its body and head. This breathing hole, which leads to a lunglike cavity, can be closed up in case of rain or attack. The genital area, beneath the mantle, is near the breathing hole.

You'll also see four tentacles on the slug's head. Small black eyes, visible on the tips of the two upper, longer tentacles, enable the slug to distinguish light from dark. The lower pair of tentacles is used to smell and taste; they help lead the slug to food and then back to its crevice home.

On a slug's menu are mushrooms, carrion, animal feces, and various plants. A mouthpart called a radula, resembling a nail file covered with thousands of tiny sharp teeth, rasps its food to pulp. Slugs themselves are eaten by garter snakes, raccoons, foxes, porcupines, and others. Many would-be predators are put off, however, by the animal's copious slime. (And, as many local children can attest, the slime of banana slugs numbs the lips and tongue of anyone audacious enough to lick one.)

Banana slugs produce various types of mucus, from slippery to tacky, for different purposes. A thick slime manufactured when the slug is under attack can gum up a predator's mouth, causing it to gag. The slug also travels on slime, a coating so protective that the animal can glide over crushed glass and so adhesive that it can climb trees without slipping downward.

Mucus also comes into play during the banana slug's elaborate mating process. Slugs are hermaphrodites (each individual has both male and female reproductive organs) and can actually mate with themselves if there is no other slug available, but a partner is preferred (and ensures genetic diversity).

When two slugs find one another, the twelve- to thirty-hour-long reproductive slug fest begins. They spend hours circling one another, occasionally licking or biting each other's right side and rearing up to slap the front parts of their bodies against one another. Eventually they cozy up next to each other so that their genital areas are aligned and continue to stimulate each other for hours. Finally, penetration takes place and the slugs exchange sperm.

After a well-deserved rest, the separation ordeal begins. Because banana slugs have surprisingly large penises, it is not unusual for one, or sometimes both, to get stuck. The slugs twist, pull, and writhe. If they are unable to separate after several more hours, they will resort to a unique phenomenon called *apophallation*—severing the penis. The slugs will take turns chewing on the offending organ(s) until they are free of one another. It's likely that the penis regrows.

Each slug soon lays thirty or more eggs in a hole or crevice. The tiny hatchlings that survive their perilous childhood grow up to travel the woods on one foot, chew with many teeth, and leave a silvery trail of slime wherever they go.

Pileated Woodpecker

Latin name: *Dryocopus pileatus*

Description: 15 inches; head has vivid red crest (in females, the front half of crest is black); head black with white; males have red "moustache"; white of underwings visible in flight; black beak.

Habitat: Most common in older Douglas-fir stands; also found in mixed coniferous and deciduous forests with large, dead standing trees.

Now that the ivory-billed woodpecker is probably extinct on our continent, the title of largest North Americn woodpecker passes to the pileated. (The ivory-billed was confined to old swampy forests of the Southeast; a very small population may yet exist in the mountains of eastern Cuba.) The pileated (pronounced either "PILL-e-ated" or "PIE-le-ated") has always maintained a stronghold in the West, although it was nearly exterminated in the eastern part of the country as its once-vast forests disappeared. In recent decades, the pileated has made a return in the Eastern states.

Its hiatus was understandable; this is a bird that needs some forest around it. The pileated requires good-sized trees to carve its large nest into and to use as roost sites. Carpenter ants, its main food, also require old wood for a home, and a mated pair of pileated woodpeckers need plenty of ants to sustain themselves and their young.

Digging out those ants and other wood-boring insects takes specialized equipment. The woodpecker finds its prey by listening for faint rustlings under the bark. Once it has targeted the grub, beetle, or ant nest, the pileated whacks away at the area with its beak, sending big fat wood chips flying. Strong neck muscles and thick skull bones absorb the shock, so the bird doesn't end up punch-drunk after a day of pounding its head against a tree. The resulting rectangular holes, some large enough to stick your fist into, are a classic sign of the pileated woodpecker.

Once the bird has drilled into an insect's tunnel, it excavates the victim with its specialized tongue. The woodpecker's large salivary glands coat its tongue with sticky mucus that ensnares insects, and the tongue is also barbed, which further helps it secure its prey. Like other members of its family, the pileated can also extend that tongue more than twice the length of its head. This is because the tongue doesn't end near the lower jaw, like ours does. A woodpecker's tongue apparatus is anchored (depending on species) near the right eye or in the nostril. It circles over and behind the brain, allowing the woodpecker's tongue to be longer than its beak. The tongue, when extended, can reach four or five inches out of the bird's mouth. A burrowing beetle hardly stands a chance.

The pileated uses its chisel-like beak for more than finding food. Drumming with its beak on a resonant limb, rat-a-tat-tatting in a characteristic style, also helps it find a mate. Either sex may drum, but unattached males tend to do so most frequently. Once a pair has mated, they usually stay relatively near each other even after

nesting season is over. In preparation for their eggs, the pair chooses a large standing dead tree and excavates a hollow that may extend almost two feet deep. The male does the majority of the work and, once the four or five eggs are laid, also does the majority of the incubating, taking not only some day duty but the entire night shift as

well. When one of the parents arrives to trade places, the sitting one taps an acknowledgment from inside the nest, before it comes out. The parents continue to feed their young after they leave the nest, and the family group stays together into early autumn.

In addition to their nest holes, woodpeckers also hollow out roosting, or sleeping, holes. Unlike most birds, woodpeckers spend every night tucked inside a tree. Pileateds tend to have several different roosts from which to choose, a trait that ties these birds in an ecological web with other forest creatures. A number of birds, such as wood ducks, bluebirds, and swallows, and mammals, such as deer mice and flying squirrels, are unable to excavate their own homes and depend on the abandoned abodes of woodpeckers. The interconnections among species within an ecological system are not always as obvious as those exemplified by the pileated woodpecker. But as long as you can hear pileateds pounding into trees, you'll know that the intricate beat goes on.

Northern flying Squirrel

Latin name: *Glaucomys sabrinus*

Description: To 17 inches, including tail; sleek, fine fur reddish brown on back, tan below; furred skin membranes stretch from forelegs to hind legs; large eyes; horizontally flattened tail.

Habitat: Old-growth forests, coniferous forests, mixed and deciduous forests, especially at forest edges along streams and rivers.

L ike most people, my closest encounter with flying squirrels has been watching Rocky (and his pal Bullwinkle) in Saturday morning cartoons. Although they are quite common, flying squirrels aren't often seen in the wild simply because they are nocturnal. Other Northwest squirrels are diurnal and are some of the most conspicuous mammals in the forest. It isn't until these chatty cousins have retired to their nests for the night that flying squirrels become active.

Unlike Rocket J. Squirrel, flying squirrels can't really fly. (Bats are the only mammals who have achieved this feat under their own power.) Instead, flaps of fur-covered skin extend from the squirrels' wrists to their ankles and allow them to glide. Launching itself from high in a tree, the animal spreads its four legs, stretching the skin flaps, and sails at a downward angle. The horizontally flattened tail acts as a stabilizer, rather than a rudder as one might think. The squirrel steers by raising or lowering a foreleg, altering the body's aerodynamic drag: dropping the right leg, for example, turns the animal to the right. At the end of the glide, the squirrel raises its tail to land facing upward on a tree trunk.

If the squirrel intends to glide on an unfamiliar flight path, it performs a rapid series of push-ups or leans far to either side before it takes off, apparently reckoning the distance to the landing place. Once it touches down at its destination, usually another tree trunk, the squirrel darts around to the opposite side in an attempt to elude predators, particularly owls. If the squirrel has farther to go, it speeds up the tree trunk and again leaps to soar through the air with the greatest of ease.

This arboreal acrobat's preferred food, rather than being sensibly located in the treetops, is instead found just beneath the soil on the forest floor. "Truffles" are the below-ground reproductive bodies of various fungi. Flying squirrels are particularly fond of truffles and, in some parts of their range, feed on them nearly exclusively.

The eating of truffles by flying squirrels is part of a larger ecological chain reaction that may link not only fungi and squirrels, but also the spotted owl and old-growth habitat. Certain kinds of fungi attach to the tips of growing plant rootlets and form a mycorrhizal (MY-co-RYE-zal) relationship. In this mutually beneficial association, threadlike structures grow on or throughout the rootlets, and these aid the plant by more efficiently absorbing water and taking up minerals and nutrients from the soil. In return, the mycorrhizal fungus benefits by receiving sugars produced by the plant through photosynthesis. Many trees—including Douglas-fir, pine, spruce, larch, fir, hemlock, birch, oak, and alder—benefit from their association with mycorrhizal fungi.

The fungi replicate by producing truffles and tend to fruit most abundantly near large fallen trees—which, of course, are typically found in old-growth forests. Flying squirrels, drawn by the enticing odor of the truffles, dig them and gobble them up. When the foraging animal later defecates, viable spores of the fungi carried in the feces can be transferred to the root tips of another tree. (Other truffle-eating animals also inoculate trees this same way.) Spotted owls enter the picture because flying squirrels make up a large part of their diet. It's been speculated that spotted owls may be attracted to old growth because flying squirrels are attracted to mycorrhizal fungi that produce fruit near big old trees.

Relatively little is known about the flying squirrel's home life compared to that of its more visible cousins. However, the female raises one litter per year of two to five young in a round nest often made of leaves. In winter, each member of the now-dispersed family seeks better-insulated shelter in a hollow tree. Regardless of season, when daylight arrives, flying squirrels are hidden in their nests. Here they snooze and rest while the other squirrel species work the day shift.

Grouse

Latin names: *Bonasa umbellus* (ruffed grouse); *Dendragapus obscurus* (blue grouse)

Description: Ruffed: to 14 inches; male has erectable black, feathered neck ruff. Blue: to 17 inches; male has yellow-orange comb of bare skin over eye. Mottled, gray-brown, chickenlike birds; in winter, small protuberances grow on the margins of the toes, helping the bird to walk on snow.

Habitat: Coniferous forests, especially those with some deciduous trees.

Something about the ruffed grouse reminds me of an onstage Elvis Presley, especially in his later years. The plumpness, the strutting, the black neck ruff extending like an upturned collar . . . If only Elvis had been a drummer, the picture would be complete.

The ruffed grouse doesn't sing to attract females, as do most male birds (and as did Presley himself, for that matter). Instead, he finds a suitable "drumming log" to act as his stage. As dusk falls, the bird climbs up on this log and parades about, stiff-legged, with tail fanned and neck ruff raised. From time to time he stops, pulls himself stiffly upright, cups his wings, and begins to beat the air. The hollow booming starts slowly at first, then builds in intensity as his wings drum faster and faster. Under ideal conditions, the drumming can be heard for over a mile. But it is difficult to know which direction the low-toned beat is coming from, even when the bird is nearby. Then the drum roll winds down, and the ruffed grouse struts until it feels inspired to repeat the performance.

The related blue grouse has a different way of proclaiming his territory and charming his prospective mates. Standing on a tree limb, rock, stump or log, the male inflates two air sacs in his throat. This expands (and shows off) the featherless, yellow patches of skin on his neck and provides the *oomph* for a series of low-toned, amplified hoots.

A female grouse is drawn by her particular species' serenade and seeks out the performer. She observes him for a time and, if she is impressed with his talents, the two will mate. Afterward, she wanders off and will eventually prepare for the eggs she'll lay, while he goes on with the show, hoping to attract another groupie.

Females of both species scrape out a depression on the ground for their eggs—often beside a log, a rock, or some other object so that, as she incubates the eggs, the female will be protected from behind. She lines the scrape with grasses and perhaps a few feathers before laying her eggs, which usually number six to eight for blue grouse and nine to twelve for ruffed.

Relying heavily on her camouflaging coloration, the female will sit tight on her nest despite the near approach of predators. When she is at last

convinced that she's been spotted, she'll break into a performance of her own: the broken-wing routine. Feigning injury, she'll lead the predator well away from her nest before making her own escape.

Male grouse will also sit quietly, blending in with their surroundings, until you nearly step on them. If you're a hunter looking for grouse, this sudden explosion makes the hunt a thrill. If you're just wandering through a field, not thinking about grouse at all, it can scare the bejeezus out of you. Blue grouse, more so than ruffed grouse, seem to take this camouflage-survival strategy to the extreme. It's possible to walk up to them and kill them with a stick as they sit out in the open on a tree limb. They're also slow to flush when along the roadside (perhaps picking up fine gravel to aid in digestion). This "What, me worry?" attitude has earned them the name "fool hen." (The spruce grouse, found most often east of the Cascades, also shares this title. Alternative names for the blue are hooter or sooty grouse; the ruffed is also called drummer; and in the Eastern states, grouse are usually called partridges.)

The occasional "crazy flight" of grouse certainly doesn't improve our impression of their intellectual powers either. The impulse for this behavior is still under debate, but the result is that a bird breaks into a rocketing, apparently oblivious flight that can take it away from the safety of cover and cause it to crash into buildings. Crazy flight apparently gripped the grouse that once whammed into the window of a Forest Service bunkhouse with a force that blasted the glass into shards, brought me running from another part of the building, and left the grouse dead on the ground outside. Some biologists suggest that this is an aberrant behavior rising out of the usual "fall shuffle," a term used to describe the annual break-up of family groups. The fall shuffle results in dispersal of the young, eventually allowing the birds to claim new territory. And a territory on which to perform leads to the low, throbbing backbeat that accompanies late spring in the Northwest woods.

Devil's Club

Latin name: *Oplopanax horridus*

Description: Stems grow up to 10 feet high, covered with yellowish spines; 6- to 15-inch-wide maple-shaped leaves covered with prickles on top and bottom.

Habitat: Along streams, in seeps, in moist woods.

Throughout the United States, many thorny or otherwise disagreeable plants are tagged as various possessions of the devil. You can find devil's paintbrush, weed, claw, trumpet, pincushion, and plaything. In moist woods and along streambanks in the Pacific Northwest, you'll find devil's club.

Take a good look at this spiky plant when you encounter it along a trail. Numerous yellowish spines up to half an inch long crowd its thick stems. Its pretty, maple-shaped leaves, which can be larger than twelve inches across, wield additional, smaller spines along their largest veins. Cautiously lift a leaf and you'll see that even the undersides of the veins are spiked. This plant is impressively armed.

It's one thing to admire the weaponry of devil's club from the relative civility of a well-established trail. It's another encounter entirely to run into it when you're bushwhacking. Maybe you're laying a survey line or doing a wetlands census, or maybe you can suddenly spot the trail you've been reconnoitering toward just beyond a fringe of devil's club. Against your better judgment, you press forward. Given its opportunity to grab you, devil's club makes the most of it. The thick spines on the stems slash as you attempt to move past, while your sleeves, pant legs—and tender skin!—are snagged by the hooked spines on the leaves. The flexible stems bend, trailing you, delaying your escape, as if the plant were holding you there for further punishment. Once mauled by devil's club, a person learns to heed the spiny warnings and take a long detour to avoid another diabolical encounter.

In spring inconspicuous, pale greenish flowers appear on a stalk at the top center of the plant. The many small, puffy flowers cluster together in a cone shape. After pollination, these are replaced by yellow berries that gradually shade into orange and, by August, a brilliant red. The conical stack sometimes leans over from the weight of the fruit. The berries are said to be poisonous, though bears apparently eat them without harm.

Despite devil's club's hazardous qualities—or perhaps because of them—it had many uses among Indian tribes, some of which extend to present day. Ethnobotanists, who study ancient uses of plants, report that shamans carved the plant's wood into powerful, protecting amulets, and built shelters of devil's club when they needed special protection. Fishing hooks and lures can be made from the wood; burnt stems mixed with grease make a reddish brown face paint. Dry, pulverized bark was used as the equivalent of our modern perfume, baby talc, and deodorant.

Because devil's club is in the ginseng family, it makes sense that the roots and green inner bark of the plant were especially important in making medicines. These were used by different tribes to treat a variety of ailments including diabetes, arthritis, rheumatism, tuberculosis, ulcers, and other stomach troubles. Far from avoiding this plant, Indians respected it and gathered it for its powerful medicine.

Perhaps because of devil's club's healing quality, the Latin root *panax*, meaning "cure," was incorporated into its scientific name. The rest of the name can be interpreted as "horrible weapon." This certainly suits the plant, as any bushwhacker who has been bushwhacked by devil's club will agree.

Red fox

Latin name: *Vulpes vulpes*
Description: 20 to 30 inches long plus 14- to 16-inch tail;
reddish coat with white underparts; black legs and feet; tail tipped white.
Habitat: Open fields that are interspersed with brush or trees.

My husband, Tim, and I were walking through classic red fox habitat—a field hemmed with trees—when one suddenly materialized out of the tall grass. He saw us too, and for a moment we regarded one another, forty feet apart. A fox is such a handsome animal: the triangular face, bright eyes, coat the color of flame, cool white belly, and singed black legs and feet. It's doubtful he viewed us with similar admiration. He turned and trotted daintily into the woods without a backward glance.

Foxes are smaller than most people expect. Excluding their tails, they are only about two or two and a half feet long, and weigh just ten to fifteen pounds. They are intelligent, clever animals—the fox who evaluated us probably deduced he had no need of a quick escape because we carried nothing resembling a rifle.

Not all red foxes have the red-orange coat that earned them their common name, although most in the Northwest do. The other color possibilities are black, silver (black with long white-tipped guard hairs), and cross (a dark streak of fur across the shoulders and down the back in the shape of a cross). All of these phases have the white-tipped tail. (There is also a gray fox, which is found in some parts of Oregon and Northern California. It has a black-tipped tail and frequents forests—where it climbs trees.) None of the Northwest's foxes turn white in winter.

Except for females who are about to give birth or who have young pups,

---

the adult fox sleeps outside rather than in a den. On chilly days, it seeks a south-facing slope or some other warm spot, where it curls up like a house cat, covering its nose with its tail. In stormy weather, the fox may shelter under drooping, tentlike evergreen branches or heavy brush.

Shortly before the sun goes down, a fox gets busy. It is generally active from dusk to dawn and does most of its hunting during this time. A fox will eat rabbits, carrion, frogs, nuts, berries, and other fruit, and is well known as a chicken-thief. But the mainstay of its diet is mice and voles. The fox is a consummate mouser. It stands motionless over burrows, as alert and intent as a dog focused on a treat—which, in fact, it is. Large ears help it discern faint rustling, and should a mouse blunder out of its burrow, the red fox makes a sudden pounce, leaping straight up into the air and coming down with front paws together to pin its prey. A fox will also dig to reach the furry morsels.

Pregnant females are not likely to dig their own dens, preferring to enlarge a burrow originally created by a woodchuck or some other animal. Foxes are thought to mate for life, although they don't remain together for the entire year. The vixen gives birth to five or six pups in the den, usually in March or April. A muted skunky smell may tip you off to the presence of a nearby den. Should you find one, however, give it a wide berth. Foxes are sensitive to human activity and will move their young to a new den if disturbed.

The vixen initially stays in the den with the nursing pups while her mate brings her food. As the pups grow older, she'll leave them to go on hunting trips of her own. The parents now regurgitate meals for their young, who solicit this by licking at the corners of the adults' mouths. While still in the den, the pups fight among themselves to determine hierarchy. The dominant pups take food from the subordinate ones—and if prey is scarce, it is the strong who will survive.

Eventually the parents lead their young on hunting expeditions. By the time they are six months old, the young are full grown and prepared to find the fox's version of the Great American Dream: a nice little mixed habitat of field and forest edge.

Kinnickinnick

Latin name: *Arctostaphylos uva-ursi*

Description: Oval leaves to 1 inch long in a low, evergreen mat; larger stems have shredding, reddish bark; bright red berries in summer sometimes persist into winter.

Habitat: Sandy soil, coarse gravel.

*f*or years I've enjoyed the name "kinnickinnick," savoring the double click of it against my tongue, all the while assuming it was a traditional local name for the plant. But the real explanation for the word is not quite that straightforward. "Kinnickinnick" was not originally a name used by any of the Northwest tribes.

Instead, it's a term reportedly used by tribes in what is now the eastern United States to refer to any smoking mixture. Kinnickinnick could have been the dried leaves or bark of many different plants, including tobacco, sumac bark, spice-bush, red dogwood, and poke plant. As they moved West, fur traders apparently brought the term with them. Hudson's Bay Company traders applied the word to the plant we recognize as kinnickinnick when local tribes showed them it could be smoked.

What the dried leaves lack in flavor, they make up for in kick. Swallowing the smoke of the plant reportedly has a stupefying, narcotic effect. Once tobacco was introduced, Indians, traders, and trappers alike used dried kinnickinnick leaves to stretch their scant supplies.

According to Leslie L. Haskin in *Wild Flowers of the Pacific Coast*, one local name for the plant was *sacacomis,* which prompted a play on words among the French traders. The Hudson's Bay Company's clerks, or *commis,* were fond of smoking the plant and carried the dried leaves in pouches or sacks. So *sac-à-commis* became a French pun on the native name for kinnickinnick.

A plant of many names, kinnickinnick is also called bearberry because bears like its bright red berries. Their penchant for the plant is also reflected in its scientific name, *Arctostaphylos uva-ursi.* Both the Greek genus name and the Latin species name translate into the same term: "bear grapes." Birds, rodents, and deer also enjoy the berries. Most people, however, reject them as mealy and rather tasteless. Some Northwest tribes did eat the fruit, but generally mixed it with other, sweeter berries or with salmon eggs. (Incidentally, the berries are said to pop like popcorn when heated slowly, but I haven't succeeded at this.)

Kinnickinnick can be found growing on well-drained soils, or sandy banks, and in exposed areas. Increasingly, it can also be found on highway embankments, in suburban yards, and in the little landscaped plots in parking lots and beside malls. A hardy plant that tolerates direct sun and cold, snowy conditions, kinnickinnick is a favored native landscaping plant. No wonder: it rarely grows above six inches, forms a steadily creeping mat, and is also quite pretty. In spring, small pale pinkish or white bell-shaped flowers appear among the plant's one-inch oval leaves. By late summer, smooth berries replace the flowers, and their pretty, bright red stands out against the glossy evergreen of the leaves. New reaching arms grow roots as the plant expands over an area, covering rocky patches and stabilizing sloping banks.

Whether as food for wildlife, as a tobacco substitute, or as a landscaping groundcover, kinnickinnick has had a long and notable history in the Pacific Northwest.

Western Red~Cedar

Latin name: *Thuja plicata*

Description: To 200 feet tall; reddish brown bark runs in vertical lines; scalelike leaves encase twigs; foliage in flat, fanlike sprays; $1/2$-inch brown cones grow upright on branch in clusters.

Habitat: Along river bottoms and moist flats, on mountain slopes to 4,200 feet.

Western red-cedar suffers from a case of mistaken identity. It is not a true cedar, which is why the written name often employs a hyphen or is compressed into the single word "redcedar." Although various other trees claim the name—including Port Orford cedar, incense cedar, Alaska cedar, and even a juniper in the eastern United States that is also called red-cedar—no true cedars are native to the New World.

Instead, all of those trees, including our lovely cinnamon-barked Northwest evergreen, are in the cypress family. This doesn't imply it's a cousin to the bony-kneed bald cypress of Southern swamps, however. In the confusing world of common names, the bald cypress is not a true cypress, just as red-cedar is not a true cedar. (Though the two species aren't related, they both like wet places: western red-cedar grows best in moist lowland soils.)

Older names for red-cedar are sometimes still used. Lewis and Clark knew it as giant arborvitae, or "tree of life." Their Nez Perce guides recommended it for use as dugout canoes, and the explorers completed their journey to the Pacific Ocean riding in arborvitae's hollowed trunks.

Western-red cedar was the Northwest Native peoples' mode of long-distance transportation. In the centuries before they had access to metal tools, the tree's relatively soft wood allowed a team of men wielding stone implements to fell even large standing trees. Through a long process of alternatively burning the interior and scraping it, the trunk was gradually hollowed out. Canoe builders then added water and hot rocks to the cavity, and the resulting steam allowed them to insert thwarts, widening the shape of the log. Bigger canoes were outfitted with masts and sails. The largest dugouts were sixty-five feet long and able to carry forty people.

And what material was used to make the sail? Again, western red-cedar. After processing, the tree's soft inner bark could be woven into sails or blankets or clothing. The Chinook and other people made many household items from red-cedar, including diapers, cradle linings, floor mats, baskets, hats, dishes, ropes, and roofing material. And cedar's remarkably straight grain made it possible to split a log into planks by driving wedges into the butt end. The tree also provided knife handles, spears, bows, arrow shafts, and line for fish nets. Religious implements and totem poles were made from it. And many parts of the tree had medicinal uses. Western red-cedar was the Northwest Coast tribes' most valuable tree species. It clothed, housed, and transported the people; it helped secure their food, maintain their health, and express their religious beliefs.

Red-cedar can live more than a thousand years; there are trees alive today that stood tall when the Indians were the only people in this land. One reason it is so long-lived is that the bark exudes a natural fungicide that makes it resistant to decay. Stumps left behind by Lewis and Clark's party in 1805 were recognizable as late as 1900. This durability, along with the wood's tendency to split easily and cleanly, continues to keep it in demand for siding, fencing, and shingles.

Unlike other conifers, red-cedar can self-pollinate and produce viable young. It is also a prodigious seed producer. Although its cones make only six seeds each, these are so small that they are overlooked by squirrels and the other usual seed plunderers. The result is that many seedlings germinate. The droopy-tipped seedlings, however, have many enemies, including birds, insects, and direct sunlight.

But once established, a western red-cedar can reach impressive proportions, adding steadying buttresses around its base as it ages. Along with those folded, fluted edges, the old cedars still standing today have gathered many names as they've grown through the centuries. Translations of tribal names include "rich-woman maker" and "long-life maker"; settlers added "canoe-cedar." Maybe some future day, western red-cedar may try on the more accurate "western red cypress" for size.

Salal

Latin name: *Gaultheria shallon*

Description: 1 to 6 feet tall; spreading shrub; reddish brown twigs with shredding bark; evergreen leaves to about 4 inches long, oval, tapering to a sharp point and finely toothed; purple to black "berries" (actually, fleshy sepal) in the summer.

Habitat: Forests, bogs, rocky bluffs, sand dunes.

Salal is a very accommodating plant. It tolerates sun, partial shade, and the ocean's salt spray. It digs its roots into soggy bogs, dry woodlands, rocky soils, glacial till, sand dunes, and nutrient-poor soils where little else will grow. Salal appeared among blown-down trees and mudflow channels near Mount St. Helens shortly after the 1980 eruption. It often grows on tree stumps and fallen logs and, in areas of extremely high humidity, can even cling to a living tree, growing as an epiphyte without access to the forest floor soil. Depending on the particular condition the plant finds itself in, it becomes a sparse, creeping shrub barely six inches tall or stretches into an impenetrable thicket eight feet tall.

That accepting nature makes salal the most common shrub in Pacific Northwest forests. These days, it may also be one of our most undervalued. The fruit of salal was once one of the most important berries in the region, especially to the coastal tribes, who gathered the purple-black berries in great quantities and prepared them various ways. In addition to being eaten fresh, they were mashed, dried, and stored in large skunk-cabbage leaves or cedar boxes. Some tribes shaped the fruit into thick cakes or loaves that weighed ten or fifteen pounds. During the long winter months, pieces of the cakes were broken off and added to soups and stews, or soaked, then dipped in whale or seal oil before being eaten.

The young, tender leaves, with their pleasant sour taste, were chewed to stave off hunger pangs or heartburn. Or they could be used as a medical dressing—chewed and then spat onto burns, boils, and sores. Dried leaves were used to treat coughs and tuberculosis.

In more recent years, salal berries have been called the "forgotten fruit" of the Pacific Northwest. Their relatively thick skins and seediness make them less attractive than huckleberries, but you might give them a try, if you haven't already. In August the berries hang plump and ready for picking, an excellent trail food. Wild-food enthusiasts praise their flavor, as do the people who still make fragrant jams or syrup, just like the early settlers. Salal berries can also be used in pies and other recipes calling for blueberries or huckleberries. (Be forewarned, however, that eating large quantities can have a laxative effect.)

From about May to June, before the berries appear, you'll find salal's small white or pink bell-shaped flowers hanging along the plant's stems among the shiny, leathery leaves. Although hummingbirds have been seen visiting the plants, the more common pollinators are likely to be bees.

Despite the numerous tiny seeds that develop in each fruit, once salal is established, it is less likely to spread by seeds than by its underground root system and new sprouts from the base of old stems. Should the aboveground part of the plant be destroyed by fire or as a side effect of tree harvesting, salal responds vigorously, sending up new shoots from its protected, intact root system.

Because the plant is so prolific and common, it isn't surprising to learn that it is ecologically important in the Northwest. The berries are eaten by bears, songbirds, grouse, squirrels, and chipmunks. Mountain beavers ("boomers") browse the entire plant, as do deer and elk—especially when other food is covered by snow in winter. They also favor the tender young leaves in spring.

Salal also makes good protective cover for the animals, and is a ground-cover of choice for gardeners who want to use native plants or to attract wildlife to their yards. It's used to stabilize sand dunes and upholster highway medians. Called "lemon leaf," it's even used by florists as greenery in bouquets. In various ways, salal continues to accommodate the Pacific Northwest's changing environment.

Douglas Squirrel

Latin name: *Tamiasciurus douglasii*

Description: To 14 inches long; fur varies from reddish to grayish brown; underside very light to dark orange; blackish stripe on sides in summer; bushy tail.

Habitat: Conifer forests, mixed conifer-deciduous forests, oak woodlands, wooded suburbs.

Douglas squirrels are the busybodies of the forest, seeming to stick their noses into everyone's business, including yours. When you walk in a forest, it's not unusual to hear your arrival announced from on high. Douglas squirrels like to keep others informed.

These squirrels are also called chickarees or pine squirrels (but so are red squirrels, a closely related species not found in Western Washington or Oregon). Their name honors David Douglas, a Scottish naturalist who tramped and canoed throughout the Northwest in 1825 and 1826. He is also the eponym for the Douglas-fir tree, which produces one of the Douglas squirrel's favored foods: the seeds contained in its cones. The squirrel also collects the seeds of spruce, lodgepole pine, grand fir, and other trees. It carries a cone to a favored eating spot, probably a branch near its nest. Here it bites off the inedible scales and extracts the seeds tucked against them. The discarded scales and cone cores fall to the ground, where a pile gradually forms. These piles, called squirrel middens, are particularly obvious when they appear beside a trail.

On your forest walks in the fall—particularly in the early morning hours—you may notice a regular bombardment of cones, coming from a particular tree. A squirrel clips off cones, which it later collects and caches for the coming hard times. In addition to being a busybody, the Douglas squirrel is a survivalist.

The cones are cached deep within a midden pile, in tree hollows, or in underground burrows, which keeps them moist and viable. The squirrel also collects mushrooms, but these need to be dried if they are to keep for the winter, so the squirrel hangs them on twigs before hiding them away in a dry place.

Additionally, the squirrel dines on what is available in season: new needles, shoots, and pollen cones in spring; fruits, berries, and insects in summer; and truffles (the underground reproductive fruiting bodies of various fungi species) whenever possible.

Douglas squirrels themselves are food for many species, including bobcats, long-tailed weasels, martens, owls, and hawks. Such tempting vittles need safe sleeping places, so squirrels have nests, to which they retire around dusk. People are well aware of birds' nests, which for the most part are used only by the incubating parents and their young. (We are often taught as children that a bird's nest is its "home," so its easy to grow up believing that birds sleep in nests each night.) Comparatively little is said about squirrel nests, which are used not only to raise babies but also as the animals' sleeping quarters.

In summer, squirrels make ball-shaped twig—or leaf—nests, usually lined with shredded bark, mosses, and lichens, where a mother squirrel births and cares for her young. The four to six babies are born in May or June and may stay with their mother until December. By then, the squirrels have usually moved to their more-insulated cold-weather nests in tree hollows. As they mature, squirrels prefer a solitary lifestyle, but with their noisy ongoing observations, they keep one another well informed of what is happening in the neighborhood.

Margined Burying Beetle

Latin name: *Nicrophorus marginatus*

Description: ³/₄ to 1¹/₈ inches; black with orange patches on wing covers; last few abdominal segments not covered by wing covers.

Habitat: Forests and nearby fields and meadows.

You don't often come across dead animals in the woods, so when my friend Carole and I came across the shrew on the trail, we stopped to look it over. Although it was limp and obviously dead, it was moving around a bit, and we realized there was something underneath it. When that something crawled up on top of the carcass, it turned out to be a shiny black beetle with bright orange markings.

Neither of us could identify the insect, nor could we figure out what it was doing. Two options seemed obvious: it should be either eating the carcass or laying eggs on it. Instead, it just seemed to be walking around on top of the thing, climbing down, and going underneath it. When it disappeared beneath the dead animal, the three-quarter-inch-long beetle was somehow able to heave about the larger, heavier shrew. We watched and wondered for a time and finally, with dusk approaching and questions unanswered, resumed our walk back to the trailhead.

That evening, a field guide gave us the name of the usually nocturnal insect: margined burying beetle. It turns out there are several different kinds of burying beetles, and the margined is native throughout North America. As its name suggests, it buries something—dead animals. The margined can entomb creatures the size of a mouse or a small bird.

A burying beetle has sensitive chemical receptors on its antennae that alert it to the presence of the recently departed. It flies to the body and examines its size and condition by walking around on it. If the body is not already lying on loose soil, the margined beetle has been known to move it as much as sixteen feet to a more appropriate place. It does this by going underneath the carcass, turning onto its back, and hooking its leg claws into fur or feathers. Then, using its six legs as levers, the small beetle is gradually able to move the much larger animal toward its ultimate resting place. As the beetle is engaged in all this activity, chances are that a suitable mate will also arrive on the scene and pitch in.

Working quickly to avoid losing their prize to maggots or larger carrion-feeders, the beetles begin to excavate the soil beneath the body. As they dig, the carcass gradually sinks below the surface and the resulting piles of loose dirt slide down on top of it. The beetles inter themselves with it. Once below ground in the crypt, the beetles are in the mood for romance. The female's act of examining and burying the body causes her already partially developed eggs to mature. The beetles mate and dig a brood chamber, where she lays her eggs. The expectant couple also further prepares the body. They remove fur or wings, moving them off to the side within the larger chamber, and shape the denuded carcass into a ball. As they work, they eat any fly eggs or already hatched maggots that they find.

By the time their own eggs hatch and are ready for food, the parents have rendered the animal's flesh edible for them by regurgitating it and depositing the resulting droplets into conical depressions on the body. The female calls her grubs to these soup bowls by rubbing a ridge on her wing covers against her abdomen. The parents tend their offspring for about two weeks, finally leaving the chamber when the young pupate. Ten days later, the transformed grubs emerge as adult beetles, ready to sniff out another dead body.

These insect undertakers are also known as sexton beetles, after the church caretakers whose duties once included burial of the dead. When, in your wild wanderings, you happen across a freshly dead small bird or animal, check to see whether it is attended by a sexton. Burying beetles do their part to give the departed a hasty burial—even if it's not one that we might consider entirely decent.

Rubber Boa

Latin name: *Charina bottae*

Description: To 33 inches long but more commonly to 24 inches;
color ranges from tannish through dark brown and olive green; purplish individuals
found in Oregon; blunt tail resembles head; small anal spurs near vent on underside.

Habitat: Deciduous and coniferous forests, clearings, clearcuts, meadows, often near water.

On a hike through a forest one day, my friend Tom spotted a length of rubber lying in a sunny spot on the trail ahead. It seemed an odd place for litter, but as he approached, the rubber slithered into the underbrush. Tom had just seen the aptly named rubber boa. The unique look of this reptile makes it unlikely that you'll mistake it for any other snake—except perhaps one of those fake rubber ones, which it strongly resembles.

Although they can be found throughout the Pacific Northwest, from sea level up to at least nine thousand feet, rubber boas are not commonly encountered because they are nocturnal, and they are apt to spend the day under a layer of forest duff rather than on top of it. So you're most likely to run into a rubber boa if you, like Tom, happen upon one that's basking, or if you uncover it while lifting rocks, bark, or logs. In addition to burrowing under things, this snake of many talents can also swim and climb trees.

And then there's its eating style: it's not named a boa for nothing. The rubber boa, like its huge tropical relative the boa constrictor, kills by coiling its body around its victim. Unlike the constrictor, the rubber boa is content to squeeze small prey like mice and shrews. It's also said to feed on salamanders, lizards, birds, and other snakes. Contrary to popular belief, a boa doesn't kill by crushing its prey but by suffocating it. As the victim breathes out, the snake simply constricts more tightly around it, and it cannot refill its lungs.

While keeping a holding coil around its prey, the rubber boa seeks out its head and begins the process of swallowing the creature whole. Snakes lack chewing teeth but do have backward-pointing teeth that help keep a meal headed in the right direction. Thanks to jaws whose right and left sides are only loosely connected (not fused like ours), the snake can alternately move each side forward, thus "walking" the prey down its gullet.

Against its own enemies, the rubber boa might emit a musk from its anal vent or rely on deception. The threatened boa will bury its head beneath protective coils while waving its tail in the air. The animal's blunt tail is shaped like its head (the rubber boa is also known as the "two-headed snake"), and it will add to the ruse by "striking" with the tail.

Like a few other snakes, rubber boas also boast very small vestigial hind limbs, called anal spurs, located near the anal vent, or cloaca. These anal spurs are one reason why biologists believe snakes had lizard ancestors. The spurs are clearly of no use in move-

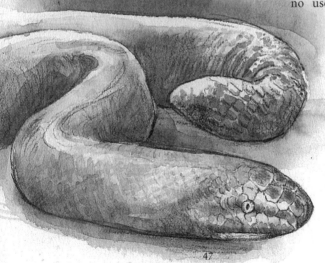

ment, but the snakes do use them in courtship. Though females are heavier and longer overall, the males have larger anal spurs, and they use these to stroke the female during copulation.

Rubber boas are viviparous—that is, the young are born live, having left their eggs while still inside the mother. Two to eight little snakes are typically born sometime from August to November. The seven-inch-long, tan or pink snakelets are on their own immediately and are rather easy prey until they grow and molt enough times to give potential predators a fair fight—or a fake strike.

Little Brown Bat

Latin name: *Myotis lucifugus*

Description: To 3½ inches long; body covered with fine yellowish brown to dark brown hair; wings are thin skin membranes stretched over a framework of arm and finger bones; membranes also between legs and tail.

Habitat: Areas near water and trees, including suburbs, parks, and forests; also roosts in caves, mine shafts, trees, and buildings.

I f you have bats in your belfry, chances are they're little brown ones. "Little brown bat" is the common name for the species that's most likely to take up residence in church belfries, house attics, or barns. (And, yes, there is also a species known as the "big brown bat.")

Little or big, bats are unique among mammals because they can fly. Although they are not as fast as birds, bats are more adept at tight maneuvering. This skill, along with their ability to echolocate, makes them exceptionally efficient predators of flying insects. Echolocation works something like sonar. The bat emits a high-frequency squeak that bounces off an object, and the returning echo informs the bat about the location, motion, and even texture of midges, mosquitoes, and anything else in its path. The calls also alert the animal to tree branches or other possible obstacles. In laboratory tests, bats detect and zip around thin wires with the greatest of ease.

Still, a homeowner who finds a bat inside the house might question the critter's navigational skills. Should you find yourself in that situation, the nicest response would be to leave the broom in the closet, open a window, and turn off the lights. The bat (perhaps a juvenile still figuring out that our giant boxes are not appropriate things to fly into) will usually be able to use echolocation, sight, or smell to find its own way out. When one summer night, this suggestion failed my sister, Ann, she captured and released the bat the same way some people remove spiders from homes: she placed a clear plastic container over the invader, which was hanging on a wall, slipped a piece of cardboard behind the animal, trapping it inside the box, and then threw the whole shebang out the window.

The squeaks the bat uses in echolocation are extremely loud, so it's fortunate for us that they are at a frequency too high for humans to hear. Once they've identified their prey, bats swoop in on the insect, sweeping it into a cupped wing and immediately transferring it to the membrane between tail and leg. Still in flight, the bat tucks its head to retrieve the morsel. It gulps down small insects on the wing but may land to consume larger ones. Although bats can also catch insects directly with their mouths, they use the wing-capture method more often.

Bats usually emerge twenty or thirty minutes before full darkness and mill about in small groups, feeding. The next time you notice feeding bats, you can test their echolocation skill. Toss up a pebble near or into the midst of the fluttering bats. A bat who notices your missile will zero in, zooming directly toward it. As soon as the animal's sophisticated echolocation informs it that this flying tidbit is inedible, the bat will pull away in search of better options. It's best to use small pebbles for your play with bats; not only do they more closely match the size of the animal's prey, but should you get carried away by your game and forget about gravity, they hurt less when they bonk you on the head.

Bat play has a limited season. Little brown bats disappear around October. They hibernate over winter, often in large, cozy groups. Although they usually will have mated in the autumn, delayed fertilization results in the females becoming pregnant in the spring. In April, the females segregate to give birth and tend their young. They often choose attics and other nice, warm human structures for their maternity colonies.

Roosting bats hang upside down, of course, but when a female is about to give birth, she takes advantage of gravity. The prospective mother hangs by her thumbs, bending her tail upward so that the membranes form a cup into which the baby is born. The pup's feet, delivered first, grab the mother's fur or foot as soon as they emerge (being born while your mother dangles from a ceiling is a risky business). The pup actually helps birth itself by pulling with its legs as the mother's contractions push it out.

Once comfortably reestablished upside down, the new mother wraps a protective wing over her suckling newborn. After about a month, the youngsters are ready for forays into the darkness; they join the adults to become the fluttering pulse of the night.

Coyote

Latin name: *Canis latrans*

Description: About 4 feet long, including tail; coat grayish to tawny, lighter underparts, shades of red on legs; black tip on tail.

Habitat: Brushy areas, suburbs, rural land, and forests, especially open ones.

My husband and I spent our honeymoon camping in the Cascades, and one night we were serenaded by coyotes. Somewhere off in the trees behind the tent, a lone coyote yapped, then stretched its voice into a wavering howl. Obviously inspired, other coyotes launched their shivering notes into the night. Tim and I fell asleep to the soulful, eerie music.

Two howling coyotes can sound like an entire pack, but since this occurred in September, I suspect we were listening to a family group: mated adults with their nearly grown pups. The young eventually leave their parents' territory in search of their own mates, while the adults tend to stay together. Coyote couples have long relationships, sometimes mating for life.

Coyotes copulate in the manner of dogs but, unlike their domestic cousins, breed only during a relatively short period of time. After mating, the pair is "tied" together: the male's penis swells inside the female's vagina for up to twenty-five minutes, during which time the male steps over the female so that they stand tail to tail. It's speculated this trait locks the sperm inside the female, making conception more likely.

In spring, the pair digs a den in a sandy bank, renovates an old skunk or fox burrow, or finds a cave or crevice in a rocky area. The size of their litter varies, increasing in response to abundant food and, interestingly, to human attempts at controlling coyote population. The usual litter is five to seven pups. Initially the male brings food to the nursing female, but eventually both must hunt to feed their growing family.

The bulk of a coyote's diet is made up of small mammals, primarily rodents and rabbits, but coyotes also eat birds, fish, reptiles, amphibians, insects, berries, and other fruits—and garbage out of suburban trash cans. Their remarkably varied diet is one of the reasons they adapt well to changing circumstances. It's also the reason many ranchers revile the coyote, believing it to be a livestock killer. Biologists, however, suggest that coyotes are more likely to opportunistically feast on dead livestock than to kill the animals themselves.

But those who know coyotes can agree they are both crafty and wickedly fast. Coyotes run faster than thirty miles per hour and have been clocked at a top speed of forty-three miles per hour. They're equally quick to take advantage of others' hard work. A coyote who happens across a badger furiously digging out a ground squirrel or other rodent is likely to sit patiently near one of the rodent's exit holes. When the squirrel finally makes its desperate break, the waiting coyote snaps it up. If any animal could smirk, it seems the coyote would be the one to do it.

Northwest Indians know all about this animal's cunning. The legendary Coyote is a brash character who tricks, bribes, and cajoles his way through both ancient and modern stories. He possesses varying degrees of good or evil according to different tribes, but Coyote the Trickster is as persistent and ubiquitous in Western Indian lore as is the animal in the flesh.

Despite bounties, trapping, poison, and other "predator controls," the coyote's range has been steadily increasing. As wolves were killed off in this country, coyotes moved into their niche. As forests were converted into croplands and suburban communities, coyotes took advantage of the newly open spaces. As dense forests were clearcut, and logging roads created links between them, coyotes learned to travel them. Unlike many other species, the coyote has managed to benefit from the activities of modern humans. It's an indication of the animal's adaptability—and perhaps also its cunning.

Chanterelles

Latin name: *Cantharellus* spp.

Description: To 6 inches high; funnel-shaped; wavy-edged top; gills run down stem from top; colors range from white to deep orange, depending on species; fruity fragrance.

Habitat: Moist, coniferous forests, especially Douglas-fir forests.

L ooking at a chanterelle mushroom growing in the woods is like seeing the tip of the proverbial iceberg—there's a whole lot of fungus below the ground that we don't see. Chanterelles are just the reproductive fruiting body (analogous to the fruit on a tree) of the fungus. The underground part doesn't resemble the mushroom we know and love, however, so don't imagine a mega-'shroom buried below the chanterelle.

Picture instead a lacy network of spindly threads so fine they cannot be seen unless many of them group together. These filaments are called *hyphae,* and the organism they form is called a mycelium. The hyphae of the mycelium penetrate soil, leaves, or wood, and the entire organism can reach massive proportions. Researchers tracking a single honey-mushroom mycelium found that it covered some forty acres and was about fifteen hundred years old.

It takes a little mind-stretching to comprehend the notion of a single fungus that, rather than being an obvious physical body that we can touch and observe, instead extends over a massive area—yet is made up of individual hyphae too small to be seen with the naked eye. But the mind-bending has just begun. The hyphae themselves have different "mating types" or genders—and many fungus species have more mating types than just the standard-issue male or female. One species, for example, has over four hundred different genders. (Talk about consciousness-altering mushrooms!)

Like other mushrooms, a chanterelle is formed when one hypha pairs ("mates") with another of a different gender. Their union eventually produces a swelling that grows and pushes up through the forest duff as the familiar chanterelle. This fruiting body initially has a tiny rounded top, but the cap hollows as it grows. Mushroom gatherers are well aware that 'shrooms seem to spring up suddenly after a rain. This is because a mushroom requires water to expand; most of its growth comes not from cell division but from the spongelike drawing in of water and the inflation of cells.

Having arrived at the surface, a mushroom's job is to disperse its spores. These single cells, tiny and plentiful, waft away on the wind. One that happens to land on a favorable site will produce a hypha, a single filament. The hypha will branch and grow to become a mycelium capable of producing more mushrooms. A mushroom gatherer who finds a choice site for chanterelles one year is apt to be rewarded by repeat visits in subsequent years, thanks to the unseen mycelium underground.

The astute gatherer knows that chanterelles are usually found near Douglas-fir trees. This is because the mycelium cannot produce its own food. Like all fungi, it relies on other organisms to supply its food. Fungi have various ways of solving this dilemma, but the mycelium of chanterelles forms a mycorrhizal (MY-co-RYE-zal) relationship with a tree, usually a Douglas-fir. The fungus attaches to the tree's rootlets, resulting in a mutually beneficial relationship: the tree creates food through photosynthesis and passes some of the sugars to the fungus, and the fungus greatly improves the rootlets' ability to absorb water and take up nutrients and minerals from the soil. This type of relationship is not limited to chanterelles and Douglas-firs; some canny mushroom hunters use their knowledge of which kinds of mushrooms associate with which kinds of trees to help them find their favorite species.

Chanterelles are worth seeking out. They rank high among the Northwest's most popular and most economically important species. Legions of 'shroom hunters comb the woods in spring and fall to gather them for their own culinary use or for profit. The Pacific golden chanterelle (*C. formosus*) is more economically important, but the white chanterelle (*C. subalbidus*) is often considered superior in flavor.

Chanterelles are recommended to beginning mushroom gatherers, not only because they are delicious, but because their distinctive appearance makes them less likely to be mistaken for a poisonous species. (It is, of course, imperative to consult a detailed mushroom field guide or other knowledgeable source before gathering or eating *any* wild mushroom.) In addition to an expanded larder, 'shroomers have an attribute useful to Pacific Northwesterners: a heightened appreciation of the rain—which, after all, is what swells the cells of chanterelles.

Turkey Vulture

Latin name: *Cathartes aura*
Description: About 27 inches; black body feathers; bald, red head; white bill.
Habitat: Open land, meadows, pastures, ranges, farmland; from sea level to alpine areas.

y human standards, the turkey vulture's lifestyle is downright revolting. There's the matter of food choice—something dead, and the more putrid the better. Then there's the bird's habit of defecating on itself, and its defense strategy of projectile vomiting. To top it all, the ungainly turkey vulture is, as described in a 1936 book called *Birds of America*, "ugly to the last degree . . ."

Indeed it is. The turkey vulture's nostrils are situated inside one large opening, as if the bridge of the bird's beak had been pierced with a chisel. From the shoulders down it's dressed in black, but its head and neck are featherless and the bare skin is colored a deep red. It's bald for a reason—so that it can dip into gooey carcasses without fouling any feathers. Lacking them, however, its head looks disproportionately small, and when the bird is soaring high above it can be difficult to see its head at all.

Still, the last part of the *Birds of America* quote is "ugly to the last degree, except in flight." In the air, the vulture's nearly-six-foot wingspan and its adroit use of thermal winds makes it one of the best soaring birds in the world. Vultures typically circle at two hundred feet or higher, rocking and tilting with the air currents. They keep a sharp eye not only on the ground below but also on each other; if one descends to a meal, others for miles around will follow.

Like eagles and hawks, the turkey vulture has keen eyesight that helps it locate its next meal. Unlike other birds, it uses its sense of smell to hone in on food. It has the largest olfactory system, which is rudimentary in most birds, and very likely the best sense of smell of any bird. Researchers once debated whether turkey vultures found dead mammals by smell and whether the stench of rotting carcasses could rise high enough into the air to reach them. Some wondered whether the vultures could also smell fish. Researchers proved the birds' olfactory talents with experiments, but one warm afternoon in the Columbia River Gorge answered all of those questions to my satisfaction.

That day, a stench along a tributary to the river was overpowering. I couldn't tell what had died—only that something had, and somewhere nearby. It was difficult to determine exactly which direction the smell was coming from. Searching initially along the riverbank, I glanced up and spotted turkey vultures wheeling above, obviously looking for the same thing I was. Given their superior eyesight and position, I wondered why they weren't already dining on the dead. Eventually, in a dense tangle of saplings a few hundred feet from the river, I found twenty or more rotting fish that someone had apparently caught illegally and dumped. As I buried the stinking carcasses, I realized that the cover of the young trees had hidden them from the spies in the sky. That afternoon convinced me that turkey vultures *can* smell their way to their next meal, be it flesh or fish.

The gas industry could also have confirmed the vultures' keen sense of smell. As early as the 1930s, workers pumped ethyl mercaptan (a foul-smelling gas) into pipes, then watched the skies for gatherings of turkey vultures to determine where the pipes were leaking.

The birds tend to dine communally, and to roost together in a tree away from human intervention. They also have group mating displays, in which the males parade and dance, hopping in a circle to impress the females. After the female chooses her partner and they mate, the two take turns incubating their two eggs, which are usually laid on bare rock, in a cave, or on a cliff ledge. Both parents also feed their young. The babies dip their beaks inside the parent's beak to slurp up a regurgitated soup. Some biologists speculate that the regurgitated food transfers antibodies to the young, making them immune to botulism and other lethal bacteria and viruses that are found in dead flesh.

Both unguarded young vultures and feeding adults are best left alone, since their mode of defense is projectile vomiting. Another off-putting turkey vulture habit, that of excreting onto its legs, has nothing to do with defense; the bird simply cools itself in this manner because it has no sweat glands.

You might pardon the turkey vulture its unsavory reputation since, after all, it performs a valuable service by disposing of dead animals, thereby reducing the chance of disease. You might even admire the big bird's soaring ability. But no matter how you feel about turkey vultures, you'll still want to keep your distance.

Indian Pipe

Latin name: *Monotropa uniflora*

Description: To 10 inches high; a cluster of stems, each ending in a bell-shaped flower; close, scalelike leaves; white overall, occasionally pink-tinged, turning black as it ages. Shaped like a shepherd's hook until seed development, when the plant stands erect.

Habitat: Moist, shady forests.

There's something vaguely creepy about Indian pipe. Maybe that's due to the plant's waxy, nearly translucent whiteness. Or because it's clammy and cold to the touch, or because, within a few hours of being picked, it turns black. Maybe it's just that Indian pipe doesn't seem to be anything we can easily categorize: it's the wrong shape to be a mushroom and seems too white to be a wildflower. Nonetheless, like a daisy or a dandelion, a wildflower it is.

But not *exactly* like a daisy or a dandelion—the *entire* plant is white, after all, which means that it has no chlorophyll and so cannot produce any food for itself. For many years people believed that Indian pipe gathered its nutrition from dead and decaying plants, but the actual story turns out to be more intricate and interesting than that.

Indian pipes are found in forests because they freeload off trees—usually Douglas-firs in the Northwest. But the small plants don't directly siphon off the tree's nutrients; they rely on an underground intermediary. The tree and the Indian pipes are connected to one another via an underground fungus. The fungus, which takes the form of long delicate threads, hooks up with the Indian pipe and also intertwines the fine rootlets of the tree. Both the fungus and the tree benefit from their association, which is known as a myc-orrhizal (MY-co-RYE-zal) relationship. The fungus helps the tree's rootlets soak up water and nutrients, while the tree passes food, which it has manu-factured via photosynthesis, to the fungus—and thereby on to the Indian pipe. Neither the tree nor the fungus benefits from its connection to the Indian pipe, but the Indian pipe cannot survive without both of them.

Because it mooches off the efforts of the tree and the fungus, the Indian pipe pops up in places too dark for other small plants to grow. Its paleness and its strange habits have long been noted, and even earned the condem-nation of some early naturalists. Consider what *Nature's Garden*, written by Neltje Blanchan and published in 1900, has to say about the Indian pipe:

> To one who can read the faces of the flowers, as it were, it stands a branded sinner. Doubtless its ancestors were industrious, honest creatures, seeking their food in the soil, and digesting it with the help of leaves filled with good green matter (chlorophyll) on which virtuous vegetable life depends; but some ancestral knave elected to live by piracy, to drain the already digested food of its neighbors; so the Indian pipe gradu-ally lost the use of parts for which it had need no longer, until we find it today without color and its leaves degenerated into mere scaly bracts. . . . No won-der this degenerate hangs its head; no wonder it grows black with shame on being picked, as if its wickedness were only just then discovered!

Other people also took note of Indian pipe's pallor and "bad habits," as shown by the plant's alternative common names of ghost-flower, ice-plant, or corpse-plant. But regardless of how people perceive it, the Indian pipe gets on with the business of its life, which basically means reproduction since it doesn't need to manufacture food. It accomplishes this the way other flowers do, by exuding a fragrance to attract pollinators and, when they arrive, collecting any pollen they already carry and smearing them with pollen before they leave. As many small brown seeds develop within the flower's bell, the "bowl" part of the "pipe" uncurls so that the plant stands entirely upright.

This detail did not escape Blanchan's notice in 1900. She ends her description of Indian pipe apparently feeling a tad more charitable toward the plant: "When the minute, innumerable seeds begin to form, it proudly raises its head erect, as if conscious that it had performed the one righteous act of its life."

Eventually that proud head bursts open to release its seeds. The ones that germinate will be those that make contact with a fungus that is well connected to a Douglas-fir. And thus will the sins of Indian pipe's next generation begin anew.

Steller's Jay

Latin name: *Cyanocitta stelleri*
Description: 11 inches; crested black head, black shoulders, deep blue body.
Habitat: Coniferous forests; mixed deciduous and coniferous woods; forest edges.

I'm not sure who compared Steller's jays to "crows in blue suits," but the description is apt. These birds are in the crow family, and like their basic-black–garbed relatives, they are raucous, bold, and intelligent.

For many people, it is the Steller's jay, not the much ballyhooed spotted owl, that is the signature bird of the Northwest forests. Its handsome color combination, curious nature, and loud-mouthed call tend to catch a camper or hiker's attention. Steller's jays are found all the way from sea level up into mountain forests. If a neighborhood has lots of large evergreen trees, they'll even reside in suburbia, demanding their share of the suet or birdseed found there.

But Steller's jays are the bullies of the backyard bird feeder. A large feeder might host over a dozen little birds—pine siskins, juncos, finches—all feeding peaceably together. When the big brash Steller's jay swoops in, all the little birds scatter.

In addition to the suet and birdseed handouts, these jays search out nuts, fruits, and weed seeds. Such food makes up the bulk of their diet, but the omnivores also eat insects and spiders and are not averse to a little carrion either. They are also known to take occasional bird eggs and nestlings—which does not endear them to backyard bird enthusiasts.

Meanwhile, the jays have their own trouble with bigger birds: they are hunted by owls and hawks. Like crows, groups of jays will "mob" a potential predator, dive-bombing it from above while screaming what sounds like the equivalent of bird obscenities. By paying attention to the uproar, you can sometimes be alerted to the presence of an owl or a hawk. The Steller's jay's more typical call, also rather harsh-sounding, is often interpreted into English as "shaak, shaak, shaak!" Steller's jays are fine mimics, especially noted for their rendition of a red-tailed hawk's scream. Less often heard is their sweet, subdued "whisper song."

The one time this bird is certain to be quiet is while it approaches its own nest. Both parents avoid calling attention to their young, usually secreted near the trunk of a conifer tree. The male and female build a bulky nest of twigs, plastering the deep cup inside with mud and then lining it with grasses, rootlets, and tree needles. The female usually lays four eggs, which she incubates for sixteen days. Both parents tend their nestlings, and the family group will often stay together for more than a month after the young have left the nest.

Many Westerners call the Steller's jay a "blue jay," which is the common name of a related eastern bird seldom seen in the northwestern part of the country. (The western scrub jay, found in Oregon and parts of Washington, is another relative that's often called a blue jay.) Our bird's common name honors the German naturalist Georg Steller, who first described it for science, along with many other species. If you're a history buff, you may recall that Steller was aboard the ship of Captain Vitus Bering, who explored the Alaska coastline in the mid-1700s; if you're more familiar with animals than history, you may recognize the name associated with the Steller's sea eagle, Steller's sea lion, and the now-extinct Steller's sea cow. Unlike the slow-moving sea cow, the quick-witted jay has fared much better from the eventual invasion that followed Northwest explorers like Bering and Steller.

Townsend's chipmunk

Chipmunks

Latin name: *Tamias* spp.

Description: To 6 inches long, depending on species; body brown; three black stripes and four pale ones run down back; stripe also from nose "through" eye to ears; furred tail.

Habitat: Coniferous forests, brushy areas, clearings, depending on species (although there is some overlap).

When I worked at Mount St. Helens National Volcanic Monument, I noticed a big difference in the behavior of chipmunks, depending on where they lived. In the deep forests, they were shy and hard to spot, but where the trees had been blown down by the force of the 1980 eruption (and where visitors were far more plentiful), the brash little characters came right up and tried to convince me to feed them. I had assumed the difference in the animals' behavior was simply a result of their degree of familiarity with people. Now that I know a little more about chipmunks, I suspect the difference was actually in the species type.

Townsend's chipmunks (*Tamias townsendii*) are the bashful type found in Douglas-fir forests and in brushy areas. You're likely to catch only glimpses of them before they notice you, squeak in sudden alarm, and flee. Yellow-pine chipmunks (*T. amoenus*) prefer open woods and clearings—or blown-down forests. They are the more outgoing members of the family, happy to make a camper's or a picnicker's acquaintance and steal whatever food they are able to carry away.

To further complicate matters, golden-mantled ground squirrels (*Spermophilus* spp.) look very similar to chipmunks, and they frequent the same open habitats and develop the same begging ploys as the yellow-pine chipmunk. I've often overheard people misidentifying the ground squirrel as a chipmunk, but there is an easy way to tell the two apart. The eyes of a golden-mantled ground squirrel are outlined in white, while a chipmunk has a black stripe that seems to pass through each eye. The ground squirrels are also a couple of inches larger than chipmunks and have no stripes on their faces, heads, or necks (although they do have a stripe down each flank).

Regardless of where they live or how they react to humans, both species of little chippers share certain characteristics. They are active from dawn to dusk, live in similar burrows, and are hunted by the same types of predators. Home for chipmunks is generally an underground burrow, though in some areas it could be a crevice between rocks. Throughout the year, but especially in autumn, the animals cache food within their snug homes to see them through the winter. In snowy areas, the chipmunks spend the winter in a torpor, rousing occasionally to eat from their stores. In areas that get more liquid than frozen precipitation, they may be seen above ground all year long, hiding out only during the worst storms. Chipmunks enjoy berries and other fruits as well as various nuts and seeds, and may also take a few beetles. The yellow-pines also claim bird eggs. In fall, both species rely on truffles (the fruiting bodies of underground fungi), which they locate by smell. During their food forays they fill their expandable cheek pouches and then hurry home to unload the groceries and tuck them away for later.

Many larger animals, in turn, find chipmunks delectable. Their main predators are probably long-tailed weasels, which can go right down into a chipmunk's snug hideaway and dispatch its owner. But hawks, owls, foxes, bears, bobcats, lynxes, coyotes, snakes, and mink, among others, have all been named as chipmunk predators.

Chipmunks breed in spring and usually have a single litter of four young in May or June. The newborns measure two to two and a half inches long and are blind and naked, with skin so thin that milk can be seen in their stomachs after a meal. They grow quickly and stay with their mother only until July or August. The young have just enough time to dig their own burrows and cache food for the upcoming winter. Whether those newly independent adults will react to you by furtively hiding behind a tree or by practically climbing up your leg in a quest for your sandwich may be determined less by where they live than by the species of chipmunk they happen to be.

golden-mantled
ground squirrel

(note ring around eye)

Mule Deer

Latin name: *Odocoileus hemionus*

Description: Body various shades of brown in summer and gray in winter; throat and belly lighter; white rump patch; males have antlers in season.

Habitat: Usually brushy edges of forests, also wet areas and suburbia if enough cover is available.

The Gifford Pinchot National Forest visitors stopped their car to watch a mother deer with twin fawns cross the road in front of them. The doe and one baby made it across, but the other baby suddenly collapsed beside the road. The mother turned to look back at it—and then she and the other fawn bounded away, disappearing into the woods!

The concerned people examined the baby animal and tried to help it stand it upright. It collapsed again. They decided the poor thing had been abandoned because it was sickly or malnourished. The visitors put the fawn in their car and drove many miles in search of someone who would know how to help the little animal.

"Are we glad to see you!" the man called from his car, just as I was locking up the visitor center for the evening. As the group piled out of the car, I was astounded to see that fawn cradled in a woman's arms. Explaining how they'd rescued it, she set the fawn down so that its delicate hooves touched the ground. The animal's twiggy legs folded under it immediately. She looked from the fawn, now laying at my feet, to me and said, "We couldn't just leave it there."

Well, yes, they could have. This healthy fawn was merely demonstrating what instinct told it to do in threatening circumstances: lie still. Had it been left alone, the doe would have returned to claim her baby. In trying to be helpful, the visitors had taken the young animal many miles away from its mother and from its best chance of survival.

Under ordinary circumstances, the deer's survival strategy works quite well. If they tried to stay all day with their mothers, very young fawns would be vulnerable to attack by predators. Instead, she leaves them behind while she feeds, though she usually doesn't wander too far away. For the first few weeks of their lives, fawns lie so very still and have so little scent that predators can walk within feet of them without detecting their presence. The mother will charge any small predator, such as a fox, that wanders too close to Bambi. If a predator more dangerous to the mother, such as a mountain lion, begins prowling about, the doe will mosey farther and farther from her young in an attempt to lead the enemy astray.

The mule deer has two races, which can be differentiated by tail color and, generally, by location. Black-tailed deer, found west of the Cascades, have tails that are dark brown or black; mule deer, found east of the mountains, have paler tails that are tipped with black. (In both races the underside of the tails is white.) The two races were once believed separate species, and some people still quibble about which name both should be lumped under. Mule deer earned their common name not through any inherent stubbornness but because their ears are large compared to those of the white-tailed deer of the Eastern states (and its subspecies, the Columbian white-tailed deer, which still exists in small populations on the west side of the Cascades).

Our mule deer, or "mulies," have evolved a different method of fleeing than the white-tails. Pursued, they may break into bounding leaps, a behavior known as stotting. All four hooves hit the ground together in a series of stiff-legged high jumps. Stotting allows a mule deer to abruptly change direction and is especially useful on uneven terrain.

From about mid-November through mid-December, bucks travel in search of does. Only dominant bucks, those which are strongest and healthiest, will mate. Both does and inferior males recognize these dominant bucks by their impressive antlers and their scent (deer release pheromones in their urine and from various glands). The following May or June, the mated does give birth to one or two young.

The visitors who brought the collapsible fawn to the visitor center could not agree on where they had found it, and we were unable to return it to the wild. It ended up sucking on a bottle at a wildlife rehabilitation center—with a couple of other unlucky fawns who had also been "rescued."

Stinging Nettle

Latin name: *Urtica dioica*

Description: To 7 feet tall; 2- to 6-inch narrow, oval leaves with saw-toothed margins; entire plant covered with fine stinging hairs.

Habitat: Moist soil of ditches, meadows, streambanks, trailsides, edges of woods, barnyards.

Consider the ingenuity of nature shown by stinging nettle's defense system: this plant is essentially covered with tiny hypodermic needles. The leaves and stems of nettles are studded with fine hairs that deliver a lingering sting if you happen to brush against them. Each hollow hair leads to its own little reservoir of stinging fluid contained in a bulbous base. The tips of the hairs are very brittle and break off with the slightest brush from a passing animal or person. The uncapped needle, having pierced the skin, injects its load of fluid, just like a hypodermic does. The fluid has been widely reported to be formic acid, the same substance that gives zing to the bites of ants and stings of bees, but this tidy explanation has been disproven. Instead, acetylcholine, hydroxytryptamine, and a histamine are to blame for nettles' nastiness. Depending on an individual's sensitivity to this concoction, it can cause red welts or white bumps and a stinging, burning pain that lasts several minutes or several hours. Even when you think the irritation is over, just brushing or bothering the aggravated area can reactivate the sting.

It's a good idea to learn to recognize nettles before they draw your attention by their own devices. Each leaf grows opposite another on the stem and is rimmed with teeth around its edge. I look for the gap of a few inches between tiers of leaves and, in the spring and summer, for the clusters of greenish flowers that dangle like little chain lamp-pulls from where the leaf stems attach to the plant. The small flowers are segregated into separate male and female clusters, and they are the only aboveground part of the plant that doesn't threaten you with stiff, piercing hairs. When in doubt, take a close look for those fine-needled hypodermics. And remember that the plant can spread by underground stems, so where you find one, you're liable to find more.

Should you blunder into nettles, you might try one of the folk remedies that suggests that the cure often grows alongside the problem. Rubbing the sting with the leaves of elderberry, curly dock, bracken fern, or thimble-berry or with the fuzz from fiddleheads is said to lessen the sting. Applying rubbing alcohol is a more prosaic solution.

But if you're looking for revenge (or just a good meal), you can boil up a pot of nettles and eat them. Boiling or drying destroys the plant's sting. The tender shoots and young leaves, eagerly gathered by leather-gloved wild-food connoisseurs, are loaded with protein, vitamin C, and iron. Nettles were a spring vegetable eagerly anticipated by settlers, who sometimes called them "Indian spinach."

Previous generations had many other uses for stinging nettles. Weavers in Scotland, Germany, and the Scandinavian countries made cloth from nettles before the introduction of linen-producing flax. Northwest

Indians, too, used the plant's fibers, especially for making a twine they fashioned into snares, nets, and fishing lines. They also had many medicinal uses for the plant.

Beer, tea, and green, red, and yellow dyes have all been made with nettles. One old cure for stopping a nosebleed calls for placing a nettle leaf on the tongue and then pressing it against the roof of the mouth; another less painful sounding cure suggests that a cloth soaked in the plant's juice and held against the nose will do the same trick. Urtication—whipping with nettles—is an ancient treatment for rheumatism and weak muscles. The stings were said to increase circulation, and, after the initial pain, the whipping brought a warm, tingling relief to sore joints and muscles.

That stinging sensation does not appear to be appreciated by wildlife, however, so nettle's defense strategy works—except against caterpillars. The caterpillars that become painted lady, west coast lady, and red admiral butterflies vigorously chomp the plant's leaves. Red admirals, especially, use nettles as their chief food source.

When I come across stinging nettle—that nuisance to be avoided—I sometimes consider how past generations regarded certain plants differently than we do. Today, stinging nettle is valued by few humans—but at least generations of red admirals continue to appreciate it.

Mountain Beaver

Latin name: *Aplodontia rufa*

Description: To 14 inches long; dark brown or reddish brown fur, somewhat lighter below; small white spot under each ear; long whiskers; short legs; long claws on forepaws; inconspicuous stubby tail.

Habitat: Prefers coniferous forests with thickets and nearby water, but can be found in deciduous forests and in clearcuts if enough cover and forage remains.

It seems odd that an animal the size of a rabbit, indigenous to the Pacific Northwest, could be completely unknown to so many people who live here. But then the mountain beaver is an odd sort of animal. The "boomer," as it's also known, is the only surviving species in the oldest known family of living rodents. According to the fossil record, it has changed little since it first appeared sixty million years ago. Another odd detail is that the boomer hosts the world's largest flea, a bloodsucker three-eighths of an inch long.

Mountain beavers are not beavers, and they are more common at lower altitudes than in the mountains. They are, however, found at elevations up to nine thousand feet, and they received their common name from miners in California's Sierra Nevada range, who observed that the animals sometimes clipped tree branches and chewed bark. Despite those beaverlike habits, mountain beavers are more closely related to squirrels. Their other common name is more accurate; boomers do sometimes make a noise that could be transcribed as "boom." (In his wonderful book, *Cascade-Olympic Natural History*, Daniel Mathews suggests that the sound is more of a "moom" or a low moan.)

One of the reasons these animals are so little known is that they are primarily nocturnal, burrowing creatures. It's certainly possible to see them above ground in the daylight, however, and more than one hiker (including me) has peered at a boomer in the rustling underbrush and wondered, "What the heck is *that*?"

Tree farmers and foresters are all too well acquainted with mountain beavers. Although these little vegetarians favor sword fern, at certain times of year they also eat seedlings and can girdle (and thereby kill) young trees. Food items are sometimes taken directly into the animal's burrow and stored, but boomers often leave piles of vegetation just outside one of their many entrances. After the fireweed, oxalis, or berry vines wilt, the animal carries them down into a humid food chamber, where the food stays moist.

In addition to the food chambers, the boomer's extensive burrow system includes a sleeping chamber with a large, comfy nest made from vegetation and often lined with salal leaves, many tunnels leading to various entrances and exits, and a chamber where the animal deposits its fecal pellets. Additional chambers might store "mountain beaver baseballs." The animal unearths these rocks or clay balls, which are about three inches in diameter, while excavating its burrow. It apparently chews on the baseballs to file its ever-growing front teeth as well as using them to close off its residence when it is abroad.

A mountain beaver never goes too far from its home, however. It tends to stay within twenty-five yards during its food forays, which may lead it up into trees to trim edible branches. The animal's longest journey is usually the one it takes from its mother's nest to find a home of its own.

Females usually birth four or five young in March or April, having mated about a month earlier. The blind, helpless babies are slow to develop, and during this time they are especially vulnerable to underground raids by minks and long-tailed weasels. After they grow into adults, a boomer's greatest enemies are bobcats, coyotes, mountain lions, great horned owls, and tree farmers with traps.

For all their anonymity, mountain beavers are a common species (too common, say the tree farmers) in any moist, scrubby westside forest. You may not see a boomer during your next forest hike, but chances are there's one right under your nose—in its subterranean burrow.

Osprey

Latin name: *Pandion haliaetus*

Description: 24 inches; white crown; dark stripe through eye; mostly white underneath, dark above, with barred wings and tail; female slightly larger than male.

Habitat: Lakes, reservoirs, good-sized rivers, bays, estuaries.

Ospreys want a home with an overall commanding view, and they prefer it on waterfront property. A mated pair builds its nest beside (or within a few miles of) a river, lake, or bay, on something tall that allows a three-hundred-and-sixty-degree panorama. Beyond those basic requirements, the pair is not picky. A massive tree, living or dead, will do, as will the top of a bridge or building, an electric tower, or an artificial nesting platform.

Nor are they particular about the material they use to build their massive nests. A tally of the junk that has been found in osprey nests includes hula hoops, fish nets, bicycle tires, rubber boots, shirts, dolls, Styrofoam cups, cornstalks, cow bones, and TV antennas. The basic building material, of course, is branches. Ospreys use large dead ones, which they selectively break off trees: they might snatch the branch in flight, or land on it briefly so their weight snaps it off—with a resounding CRACK!—and then wing away with it.

These birds build a substantial nest. The average size of an osprey nest is five feet across, with an inside depth of two or three feet. (If it has been used year after year, it may be up to seven feet high, although the inside cup stays about the same size.) One of these behemoth homes can weigh half a ton.

The nests are often noticed not only because they are so large and conspicuously placed but also because ospreys tolerate close-by human activity. I once watched an osprey plunge into a river after a fish, surprisingly close to a group of kayakers. Because the bird had come from behind them, the kayakers weren't aware it was there until its sudden splashdown. Their faces registered astonishment as the big bird labored back up in the air with a fish gripped in its talons.

Although the osprey will take rodents, birds, and other small creatures, it is called the fish hawk for good reason. It patrols from thirty to one hundred feet above the water, watching for slow-moving fish a few feet below the surface. When it sights an appropriate target, the bird dives from the sky, swinging out its talons just before it plunges into the water. The osprey may be almost entirely immersed for a moment before powerful thrusts of its wings pull it free. Misjudgments can be fatal: ospreys have been known to break a wing on impact or to drown by locking their talons onto a sturgeon or salmon too heavy to lift. A successful bird, once airborne, shifts the fish so that it is carried head first, which cuts wind resistance. Sharp, hooked talons and roughened, spiky pads on the bird's feet help maintain a good grip.

The osprey that surprised the kayakers was most likely a male providing for his family. Much of the activity we observe during the time the birds are in the Northwest (from April to November) centers around raising young. Ospreys breed in the Northwest but migrate as far south as Chile and Argentina for the winter. Immature birds usually remain there until they are three years old and ready to mate.

The birds tend to return to old nest sites, males arriving first. He claims his territory with what has been called a sky-dance: hovering several hundred feet above the area, steeply diving and swooping back upward. The returning female, drawn back to her old territory, is apparently charmed by his fancy wing-work. He also proves his ability to provide food by repeatedly bringing her fish. Copulation is brief but may occur fifteen to twenty times a day for three weeks.

The male continues to feed the female as she broods her three eggs. As the chicks grow, the male brings food to them as well, which the solicitous mother tears into appropriate-sized offerings. The young birds leave the nest after about seven or eight weeks. Although they know instinctively how to fish, they may continue to be fed for several weeks while they master the technique. Once they migrate, we're unlikely see the young birds again in the Northwest until they are mature adult ospreys, seeking waterfront property.

Bedstraw

Latin name: *Galium* spp.

Description: To 6 feet high; square stems, 4 to 8 leaves arranged in whorls around the stem; small white flowers; most sprawl rather than stand upright.

Habitat: Moist woods, meadows, fields, trailsides, marshes.

My friend Esther and I were walking on a forest trail when she stopped to pick a low-lying plant—and then flung it at my shirt, where it stuck. That's how I learned about the clinging, Velcrolike quality of bedstraw. If you try to pluck some plant species, they will resist with every fiber of their being, but bedstraw's reproduction strategy runs to the opposite extreme. Its stem sections are ridiculously loose-jointed and let go at the slightest tug. The square stems have tiny downward-pointing hooks running along the entire length of each edge, and the leaves and small round seed cases also sport teeny hooks. These barbs grab hold of any passing animal—including the two-legged hiking kind.

I had plucked bedstraw's little spherical seeds (often called beggar's lice or beggar's ticks) out of my wool socks for years before I noticed the plant that had been sticking them on me. This thin, delicate, viney-looking plant typically lies prostrate over other vegetation and can be easily overlooked. Still, a plant that boasts over fifty common names (including cleavers, goose grass, catch weed, scratch weed, burrhead, cling-rascal, and grip grass) shows that others have been paying attention to it.

Pioneers used bedstraw as stuffing in their mattresses, which gave the plant its most common name. It seems as though it would require an awful lot of the spindly herb to stuff bedding, but perhaps its ease of gathering helped make it popular. Also, the hollow, collapsible stems stayed flexible after they were dried. And some species, when dried, smell pleasantly of vanilla or hay and were said to repel fleas.

But the plant had many other uses, here and in Europe. (Some species of bedstraw are native to the Northwest; others were introduced.) It was used by cheese-makers to curdle milk, and brewed as tea to remove freckles, treat sunburn, or improve the complexion. The young shoots can be steamed and eaten like asparagus and were used in a dish called Lenten pottage. They can also be added to salads.

Bedstraw's inconspicuous white flowers bloom from May through June. Short stalks grow up from where the leaf whorls attach to the plant's stem; these stalks branch into threes, each of which produces a small flower. After pollination, the flowers develop into sticky, burrlike pods containing two seeds each. The seeds can be gathered when still greenish, roasted in an oven until brown, and then ground like coffee beans. Since bedstraw is related to the coffee tree, it is said to make one of the best wilderness caffeine-free coffee substitutes.

Despite its many uses, bedstraw has attributes that are annoying when found in humans: it is a weak, clingy straggler that leans heavily on others instead of standing up for itself. But the natural world judges success only on the basis of continued survival and replication. And bedstraw's reproduction strategy of grabbing the nearest passerby for a free ride shows it to be a resourceful traveler and exceedingly good at delegating responsibility.

Maidenhair fern

Latin name: *Adiantum pedatum*

Description: About 20 inches tall; dark stem splits into 2 curving branches; smaller branches radiate off each stem, bearing thin, oblong leaflets that are fringed along their upper edges.

Habitat: Shady, moist areas, especially near streams or waterfalls.

Apparently I am the only one who thinks that the stalks of maidenhair ferns are purple. Field guide after field guide informs me that the stems are a shiny black, but I've always thought they looked a very deep purple, in luscious contrast with their green leaves.

At least I'm not alone in my appreciation of these ferns. Their standout difference in appearance from our other ferns and their delicate quality makes them a favorite with many people. No doubt there are some like me who, when encountering the first maidenhair alongside a trail, can't resist touching those cool, soft leaflets. I like to gently grasp one of the plant's splayed fingers to feel the feathery leaflets slide against my palm and fingers.

There's a debate over why the fern is named "maidenhair." Some references say it's because the fern's leaflets bear a resemblance to the leaves of the ginkgo, or maidenhair, tree. Others claim it's due to those shiny "black" stems or, perhaps more feasibly, the plant's skein of fine dark roots. The scientific name is more easily interpreted. *Adiantum* means "unwetted": the leaflets shed rain like Gore-Tex. The species name *Pedatum* means "bird-footed," and refers to the spread-out shape of the leaves.

The fact that ferns lack both flowers and seeds puzzled the ancients. Old

World folklore claimed that ferns once had flowers, but when they failed to bloom as did the other plants in the baby Jesus' cradle, they lost the privilege thereafter. Other legends claimed that ferns did set seed, at midnight on Midsummer's Eve, and anyone who managed to capture the seeds would be rendered invisible.

The less-romantic reality is that ferns have a two-stage reproduction process. During spring and summer, the plants form microscopic spores. In the maidenhair, these develop on the undersides of its leaflets, protected by a bit of rolled-over leaf. When mature, the spores waft away on the wind. If a spore gains an appropriately moist landing spot, it produces a tiny, heart-shaped, paper-thin plant called a *prothallium* (or *prothallus*). This new generation has a different way to reproduce: it produces both egg and sperm. The slightest film of water allows the sperm to swim to the egg and fertilize it. After this union, the next generation rises up from the prothallium. As the first tiny leaves of this new plant grow and it sends down roots, the prothallium dies. The offspring eventually develops into the plant we recognize as maidenhair.

In this method of reproduction, called alternation of generations, the offspring resembles its grandparent, not its parent. Much more ancient than the flower-and-seed arrangement used by modern plants, the alternation of generations allowed the ferns to flourish long before bees and other pollinators buzzed the planet.

Eons after the fern's debut, people showed up and found uses for the plants. Here in the Pacific Northwest, maidenhair ferns had many applications. Warriors reportedly chewed the plant's leaves to stanch internal bleeding. The Quinault and Makah used the dark stems to form lustrous patterns in their woven baskets. Berries were laid to dry on leaves of the fern that had been strewn onto cedar strips placed over a fire. Later the dried leaves could be easily winnowed from the berries. Some tribes soaked maidenhair leaves in water and then applied them to their hair; others burned the leaves and rubbed their ashes into the hair to keep it healthy and shining. Although it would seem logical, no text I've found suggests that maidenhair received its common name from this practice.

In any case, the name suits the plant. The feel of the fern's leaflets is fine and soft, like a young girl's hair, and "maidenhair" sounds quaint and romantic—most appropriate for a plant found tucked in the deep, moist, shady recesses of a forest.

Steelhead

Latin name: *Oncorhynchus mykiss*

Description: To 3 feet long; silver overall in ocean; pink or reddish
streaks along either side in fresh water; juveniles have dark green backs with
small dark spots and blue marks down side of body.

Habitat: Rivers and lakes; steelhead migrate to and from the ocean.

Although it may not seem so to the person who has fished for both, rainbow trout and steelhead are the same species. The feisty steelhead are wild and oceangoing, while the more docile rainbows spend their entire lives in fresh water.

The "rainbow" is the pink or reddish streak that runs the length of the spawning fish. Steelhead are silvery in salt water, but upon reentering fresh water they gradually regain color. The females tend to remain more silvery than males, but both show pink or red stripes and colorful cheeks.

Because they do not necessarily die after spawning and may return to mate again, steelhead were believed to be related to the Atlantic salmon, which displays this same trait. But molecular tests have reclassified them as more closely related to the Pacific salmon. Like salmon, steelhead trout are obliged to make the arduous spawning run from the ocean to their fresh-water natal stream.

The homing ability of a steelhead is still not completely understood, though it is known that the fish can smell the unique chemical and mineral odors of their birth stream. Steelhead congregate near the mouth of the river this stream empties into, and when the time is right begin their journey back home. It may take them weeks to complete their run. When they reach their specific spawning stream, the males watch the females carefully for signs of readiness to mate. The females cruise about looking for just the right area in which to make their nests, called redds.

When she has found an appropriate place, a female turns on her side and whisks the gravel with her tail. This inspires the male to begin his courtship display. He quivers and changes position from one side of the female to the other by crossing over her back. This activity may go on for hours, during which time he will rush at any other males who venture too near.

The female's beating of the gravel dislodges only a few stones at a time, and she will dig a pocket from sixteen to eighteen inches deep. When she is satisfied, she positions herself above the pocket and the quivering male takes his place beside her. The pair arch their backs and release eggs and milt simultaneously. Hundreds of compressed orange-red eggs swell as they contact the water and the fertilizing milt. The female now moves upstream and again beats the stream bottom. This action both covers the eggs and begins the next nest. She will dig and spawn in several nests, with different mates, depositing eight hundred to one thousand eggs each time.

The majority of steelhead die after mating, but some will return to spawn another season or two. The longevity record is held by a tagged nine-year-old male who returned to spawn four times.

The eggs hatch in four to seven weeks, and the young steelhead will remain in their natal stream for two years. Before they enter the ocean, the fish undergo a physiological change called smoltification. In this process, their external skin layers change so that the steelhead can survive in the ocean (a juvenile placed in salt water before it had smolted would die). The fish that manage to survive a childhood fraught with predators will eventually float downstream, tails first. They spend the next two to five years in the ocean, until the undeniable inner urging brings them home again.

Beaver

Latin name: *Castor canadensis*

Description: To 4 feet long, including tail up to 18 inches; dark brown fur; tail flat, scaly, and hairless; small eyes and ears; webbed hind feet; orange front teeth.

Habitat: Streams, rivers, ponds, lakes, and marshes.

Historians would agree that a large rodent led the way to Western expansion of the United States and Canada. In the waning years of the 1700s and the first half of the 1800s, the pursuit of valuable beaver pelts pushed much of the exploration and early settlement of unknown western territory. For several decades, the pelts were the continent's most valuable export to Europe. In addition to use in fur coats, robes, and trimmings, the underfur of beavers was pounded into a superior felt used in gentlemen's hats; that fad lasted until beaver became scarce and silk hats came into vogue.

Dead beavers may have provided the impetus to exploration, but living beavers shaped the land itself. North America's largest living rodent was once so numerous that virtually every pond, stream, river, or other suitable waterway hosted at least one colony. Through their impressive engineering skills, beavers transformed dry land into ponds, flooding out some species and creating habitat for numerous others. Eventually, when the ponds filled with silt trapped by their dams, the animals moved on, leaving behind meadows and fertile soil.

Although their numbers are now sorely diminished, a newly established beaver colony still has an awesome impact on the land. As their population rebounds, this increasingly brings them into conflict with humans who have already claimed the area.

Beavers are driven to create wetlands as a safe haven for themselves and their families. On land, they are slow, rather ponderous creatures that could make a fine meal for large predators like bears or mountain lions. Their young are vulnerable to a range of predators from great horned owls to coyotes. But in the water, adults are safe, and, with the exception of attack by otters, their young are as well. No wonder beavers are genetically programmed to react at the sound of escaping water and plug up the leak.

Beavers are vegetarians, and everyone knows they eat trees. Fewer people realize it is the thin, growing, inner layer of bark of mostly deciduous trees that the animal feeds on, along with leaves, twigs, and buds. The skinned limbs and logs are then used in building and repairs. Beavers' diet also includes skunk cabbage, some berries and ferns, fungi, pond-lilies, and algae. During the fall, beavers are eager to store food for the coming cold winter. They stick branches into the muck at the bottom of their pond, where the wood keeps nicely and is accessible even if the pond freezes over.

It's often assumed that beavers deliberately cut a tree so that it falls into the water, but it's really just a matter of luck. When trees fall the wrong way, the beavers can sometimes shove them into the water anyway. But around a beaver pond, it's possible to find felled trees that proved unmovable, toppled ones that are hung up in another tree's branches, and big trunks that were gnawed only partway through before the beaver realized it had bitten off more than it could chew.

Several adaptations aid the beaver's aquatic lifestyle. Valves close off the animal's ears and nose when it dives. Transparent membranes, similar to eyelids, protect the beaver's eyes from floating debris. Lung capacity and economical use of air allow it to remain submerged for fifteen minutes. Skin flaps that seal behind the front teeth let the animal carry branches in its mouth. And special glands near the reproductive opening of their bodies exude a waterproofing oil, which the beaver transfers to its fur with its forepaws.

Beavers are thought to mate for life, and the couple shares its lodge with not only the current year's three or four kits but also the surviving young from the previous year. The extended family's home can be the classic dome planted out in the middle of the water, a similar aboveground home on the bank, or an underground burrow in the side of the bank. In all cases, the inner part of the home is high and dry above the waterline, while its access tunnel is located underwater.

Beavers are often cited as second only to humans in their ability to transform habitat. If you want to erect a skyscraper or pour yet another asphalt parking lot, hire a human engineer. But if you'd prefer to transform a stream into a pond or reclaim a wetland, leave it to beavers.

Rough~Skinned Newt

Latin name: *Taricha granulosa*

Description: 6 to 8 inches long, including tail; bumpy back can be various
shades of brown or reddish brown; yellow to orange underside.

Habitat: Ponds, lakes, marshes, stream edges, and nearby forests.

When I discovered a rough-skinned newt on a trail one day, I figured I'd help it out. After admiring its wide grin, I carried it to a trailside stream and released it at the edge. If I'd known more about rough-skinned newts, I'd have set it back down where I'd found it—and then washed my hands in the stream. I now know that these salamanders don't usually live in the water—and that they can secrete a toxin.

Because I'd often seen them swimming in lakes or slow-moving water, I made the mistake of assuming they were mainly aquatic animals. In fact, the adults spend most of their lives on land and return to their home stream or ponds to reproduce.

Thanks to their tendency to travel in daylight, they are the salamander (newts are generally distinguished from other salamanders by their rough-textured skin) most often seen in the Pacific Northwest. Their coloration, brownish above and orangish below, also makes them easy to recognize.

If disturbed, the animal arches up both head and tail to show that pumpkin-bright belly as a warning. If it is attacked anyway, its granular skin releases a poisonous secretion sufficient to kill most animals foolhardy enough to eat one.

Humans are not immune to their toxin. Although it's hard to imagine anyone actually eating a newt, it's reported that campers who had inadvertently boiled one in their coffeepot died after drinking the coffee. Both because you'd have to seriously insult a newt before it released the poison and because the toxin cannot penetrate our skin, handling a newt is unlikely to affect you. But to avoid all chance of passing any poison from your hands to your mouth or to your food, it's smart to wash your hands after handling a rough-skinned newt. (It's also kind to get your hands wet before picking up a newt, as with any amphibian.)

This animal's one known predator is the Northwestern garter snake, which is apparently unaffected by the poison. Newts themselves dine on amphibian eggs and larvae, tadpoles, aquatic invertebrates, insects, worms, and small slugs.

Depending on climate and elevation, newts head for their watery breeding sites from December through July, sometimes traveling in large numbers. It's believed they smell their way to the streams they were born in, and may also orient themselves to the sun's position.

Males arrive at the breeding sites before the females, and undergo a transformation there. Their dry, bumpy skin becomes moist and smooth, their tails flatten, their cloaca (a vent on the animal's underside that is the common opening for the digestive, excretory, and reproductive tracts) enlarges, and rough, dark "nuptial pads" develop on their feet and hind legs. The nuptial pads help the male embrace the female during their slippery underwater courtship. He entices a female by clasping her from above, stroking her with his hind legs, and rubbing his snout across hers. He deposits a spermatophore (sperm packet) on the pond bottom in front of her, and if he has successfully wooed her, she picks it up with her cloaca.

Fertilization occurs internally, and the female lays her eggs one at a time, attaching them to submerged plants throughout the pond. The young, which hatch in twenty to twenty-six days, will feed on small aquatic insects. If they hatch late in the year they will overwinter as larvae, but those that hatch in summer undergo a gradual metamorphosis into adults, who will leave their aquatic home for terrestrial adventures.

Nowadays I realize newts know more about their lives than I do, so after picking them up, I always return them exactly where I find them. And then I wash my hands.

Lichens

Latin name: *Usnea* spp.

Description: Up to 20 inches long, depending on species; pale-green to gray-green, wispy strands; a strand pulled gently apart reveals a stretchy white core.

Habitat: On the bark of tree trunks or branches; low to mid-elevations.

I'm occasionally asked if "Lichen" (pronounced "LYE-kin") is my real last name. My answer is, "Yes, my husband and I chose it when we married." Rather than using only one of our last names, or combining them (which would have resulted in the unwieldy "DeLano-Hutchison"), we decided to choose a new family name.

But making that unconventional decision was easier than deciding what that new name should actually be. The answer finally came to Tim and me just a week before our wedding, as we walked on a favorite old-growth-forest trail. When we, as naturalists, had led groups of people through this forest, we'd point out the wisps of old-man's-beard that festooned tree trunks or pick up a piece that had fallen from the branches high above us. To help explain that a lichen is the combination of two organisms, a fungus and an alga, we would tell the story of Freddy Fungus and Alice Alga. Holding aloft a lichen, we explained that Fred Fungus could provide the structure for a home while Alice Alga could produce food, so these two organisms decided to live together. It seems they took a likin' to each other.

That old naturalists' chestnut pretty accurately sums up the symbiotic (mutually beneficial) relationship between the two organisms that come together to form one. In addition to shelter, the fungus component also provides a chemical defense against possible predators. But since it lacks chlorophyll, the fungus relies on the alga's ability to use sunlight to convert carbon dioxide and water into food.

Old-man's-beard is one of the most noticeable lichens in our forests, but there are many thousands of species of lichens, and they are found worldwide, from the Arctic to the tropics. In addition to the wispy branching tendrils seen in the various beard species, lichens can look like thin spreading crusts, scaly coatings, leafy arrangements, or little upright stalks or branches. Various lichen shapes have been compared to goblets, golf tees, heaps of salad, moss, matchsticks, coral, and miniature trees.

The lichen lifestyle is clearly a successful one, but it does raise the question of how two organisms, acting as one, replicate themselves. The most common way is simply for a piece of a lichen to break off and land in a favorable location. This piece may be a nonspecific part of the lichen that just happens to break off. But a lichen can also raise a little outcropping called a propagule (as one of our botanist friends likes to call our daughter, Hallie), which is designed to break away from the parent. Lichens can also propagate by fungal spores, released on the wind, which carry or collect algal cells.

Once established, lichens are hardy organisms, able to withstand drought, freezing temperatures, and even radioactivity. (Arctic species such as "reindeer moss" passed on the dangerous fallout from atmospheric atom bombs and the Chernobyl nuclear plant disaster to lichen-eating reindeer, and from there to the people in Lapland who eat reindeer meat. The result is that Lapps have a higher concentration of radiation in their tissues than any other people. The lichens collected the fallout because they consume airborne solids.) Although radiation apparently does not harm them, lichens are intolerant—to greater or lesser degrees, depending on species—of carbon dioxide pollution. Scientists who have charted the sensitivity of various species use this information as a local guide to monitor levels of air pollution. No lichens at all can grow in badly polluted areas. Old-growth forests, like the one in which my fiancé and I realized what our new last name should be, are lush with them.

Tim and I liked the symbology of two separate beings coming together as one, and we liked the images of fresh air and hummingbird nests that lichens invoke. Other than an unsettling moment for my mother during the explanation of our new name in our wedding ceremony (she mistakenly thought we'd taken on the name "Fungus"), the switch to our chosen name has been an easy one. You might even say our family name has grown on us.

Bobcat

Latin name: *Lynx rufus* or *Felis rufus*

Description: 2 to 4 feet long; ears slightly tufted; ruff surrounding face; body yellowish tan or reddish tan in summer, with dark spots, grayish in winter; short tail, to 6 inches long; paw size proportional to body (the similar lynx has very large hind feet in comparison to body size).

Habitat: Brushy areas, open and dense forests, occasionally clearcuts.

Considering how rare it is to see a wild cat, it's surprising to learn that there may be more bobcats in the United States now than there were in colonial days. Like the coyote, another comeback kid, bobcats are extremely adaptable; they can live in wetlands, deserts, mountains, or lowlands. They also live comfortably on the fringes and wild bits surrounding cities and suburbia.

Of the three wild cats found in the Pacific Northwest, the bobcat is by far the most numerous and widespread. It was not targeted for eradication as was the cougar, and has always enjoyed a wider range than the lynx, which is found in Alaska, in Canada, and occasionally in Washington's northernmost Cascade Mountains.

Although bobcats are fairly abundant, the reason they are seldom seen is because they don't want to be. Small, stealthy, and reclusive, they can easily avoid detection. It's a good bet that if you have spent any time in the wild, bobcats have seen you more often than you've seen them. One researcher watched a bobcat leave a forest trail as two hikers approached; he expected the cat to flee, but instead it simply sat down behind a bush, waited until the interlopers had passed, and then reclaimed the trail.

It's not just people who get the cold shoulder; bobcats also generally avoid other bobcats. To help them stay away from one another (or find each other during mating season), the cats leave messages along their regular routes of travel. These, in the form of urine and feces, can reveal interesting gossip such as a cat's gender, its readiness to mate, and how recently it was in the area. Feces, more or less covered with duff, are often deposited alongside a trail or on a slightly elevated place. Urine or feces may be included in a scrape—an area where the surface dirt or snow has been pawed into a rough rectangle. Scrapes might be topped off with scent from the bobcat's anal glands.

With the help of such information, a bobcat can establish a home range that might overlap those belonging to members of the opposite sex, while avoiding the home ranges of members of its own sex. In midwinter and spring, a male is also kept apprised of when neighboring females come into estrus and are willing to accept his advances.

After mating, the male doesn't linger long before he's off catting around again. About two months later, the female, having chosen a den in a hollow tree or log or among rocks, gives birth to three or four kittens. Initially blind and helpless, the kittens grow rapidly but will stay with their mother until fall, when, though only partially grown, they will have learned how to hunt and will be ready for the loner lifestyle.

One reason why the bobcat is thriving is that it is an opportunistic feeder. Rabbits and hares are a staple of its diet, but it also takes birds, reptiles, bats, and small rodents of all kinds. A bobcat will sometimes even tackle deer, usually when the larger animal is bogged down in deep snow.

A bobcat's main predators are human—trappers and hunters, who use specially trained hounds. When cornered, the ferocity of the small cat is legendary. This explains why the retiring bobcat, which goes out of its way to avoid people, is also known by the name of "wildcat." Under ordinary circumstances, a more appropriate name might be "mildcat."

Beargrass

Latin name: *Xerophyllum tenax*

Description: Tussocks of coarse, evergreen, grasslike leaves to 3 feet high; many creamy small flowers atop a single thick stalk that stands up from the center of the tussock.

Habitat: Meadows, fields, open forests; relatively dry areas at mid- to high elevations.

Each spring, when I returned to my seasonal duties at Mount St. Helens National Volcanic Monument, I casually noted scattered clumps of beargrass in the area south of the mountain. The open forests there had not been blown down in the 1980 eruption, and it was ideal habitat for the plant. Perhaps one or two visitors might ask about the grassy-looking tussocks if they were in flower, but they went largely unnoticed.

Then, one year, it was as if a secret message had been passed along via underground rhizomes during the winter: *Psst! We all bloom this spring. Pass it on.* Hundreds of beargrass clusters shot up stalks of flowering rocket ships. The visitors and I were surrounded by the white plumes, hoisted high. *Everybody* asked about the plants.

Before that spring, I hadn't known that beargrass characteristically flowers en masse, or that it's related to a famous desert denizen that flowers so rarely it is called the century plant. Beargrass doesn't take its flowery celebrations to such extremes, however. Depending on where the plants live and on other environmental conditions, big blooms occur every few years. And when they do, it's as if a quiet nation had suddenly proclaimed its territory by unfurling creamy white banners far and wide.

Much of the joy of nature is found in the details. The next time you notice beargrass in bloom, take a moment to closely examine its cluster of numerous small flowers, or inflorescence. Look at one of these individuals and you might recognize the familial resemblance to lilies in the long, slender stamens that jut from each tiny saucer-shaped flower. Early in the season, the inflorescence is tight and round, with the newest flower buds shaped in a nipple on its top. As it matures, the inflorescence gradually elongates, eventually stretching out perhaps a foot or so along the stem.

But some people are less interested in the blooms than in the narrow, grasslike leaves from which the flower stalk arises. When dried in the sun, these leaves turn a creamy color and become tough and wiry. Beargrass was once an important part of tribal trading commerce: the leaves were used to weave pouches, capes, and baskets, including watertight cooking baskets. Another common name for beargrass is Indian basket grass, and some basket weavers today still seek out the plant.

People are not the only ones who find good use for beargrass. Various animals, including deer, squirrels, chipmunks, and pikas, dine on it. And at least half of its common name is accurate: although it is not really a grass, bears do eat it.

The year after that magnificent bloom at St. Helens, the beargrass display was disappointing by comparison. But that was hardly surprising. After the plant sends up the inflorescence, the flowers, stalk, and clump of leaves all die. Before this happens, though, the plant creates seeds in oval capsules and sends out thick, woody rhizomes underground. Some of the seeds eventually take root and grow, and the rhizomes sprout new aboveground tussocks. In a few years, beargrass will be ready to throw another party, with hundreds of white flowers ballooning into the air.

Elk

Latin name: *Cervus elaphus*

Description: 7 to 9 feet long, 5 feet high at the shoulder; brown or tan with yellowish rump patch; shaggy neck mane; males have antlers in season.

Habitat: Coniferous forests, meadows, valleys, mountains, foothills.

Remarkable things sometimes happen to people who spend time outdoors. One March, my friends Ralph and Celese were driving through Washington's Cedar River Watershed, where they work, on their way to meet with a school group. Ralph braked the car when they spotted an elk with magnificent antlers crossing the road ahead of them. It was the time of year when elk shed their antlers, so Ralph hollered through the windshield, "Hey! Shake your head!"

The obliging elk bucked, then shook his head. His antlers fell off, one after the other, and landed in the middle of the road. Apparently startled by the sound they made hitting the pavement, and perhaps by the sudden loss of their weight, the bull raced off into the woods.

Ralph and Celese took just a moment to look at each other, wide-eyed and slack-jawed before scrambling out of the car to collect the antlers. They each hefted an antler and exclaimed over its impressive size and branching six-pointed spread. The base of each was somewhat moist and spongy and ringed with spots of blood. Still standing in the middle of the road, Ralph and Celese held the massive antlers in their hands and called their thanks into the forest.

The elk didn't need its antlers anymore because they'd already fulfilled their purpose the previous fall—that of advertising the animal's vigorous health and preparedness for battle. Antlers are bones that grow covered by a thin layer of skin, the "velvet" that dies and is sloughed off before mating season begins. Their size and structure reveal the elk's age and whether it has received good nutrition. Old, sick, or injured bulls grow small or crooked antlers. The size and symmetry of the pair of antlers that Ralph and Celese now use in their educational programs show that they came from a strong, mature, robust male. The stately headgear weighs in at what would seem like a neck-bending thirty pounds.

Bulls have additional ways of broadcasting their physical prowess. One of the better known is bugling. This resonant sound begins with a low note that rises to a high-pitched whistle, accompanied by a deep-chested bellow. The whistle carries long distances and the bellow indicates the animal's size: the lower the pitch, the broader the chest that created it. The animals recognize one another by their distinctive calls.

The haunting bugles that ring through elk country from September through October can raise the hair on the back of a person's neck. Less romantic as far as human sensibilities are concerned are pit-wallowing and urine-spraying. The scent of the male's urine carries information similar to that revealed by his antlers; it might notify both cows and other bulls that he is so well conditioned he is metabolizing fat, or that he requires fresh food to keep up his strength—or that he is reduced to converting muscle.

The bull shares this information with the world by wallowing in a pit of his own urine and by spraying himself on the long hairs of his neck and belly. Like a garden hose with an adjustable nozzle, the elk can control the shape and aim of his urine, misting it onto his belly or directing it in a stream between his front legs and onto his lowered neck. All of this information may help bulls avoid conflict by announcing which of them is more robust. It also helps intrigue the target of their advertisements, the cows.

Male elk attempt to collect as many mates as possible. Although a bull can be brusque and belligerent when herding cows into his own private harem, he is solicitous when it comes to copulation. A courting bull approaches the female, flicking his tongue in and out. If she allows him to, he will lick her all over, especially when she is at rest. If she is not interested in his advances, she moves away from him, holding her head low and shaking it from side to side as she opens and closes her mouth. At this signal, the bull stops; the female controls the timing of copulation. He regularly courts the members of his harem in this way. When a cow enters estrus, she allows him to mount her and mate. The resulting young, usually one per cow but occasionally twins, are born in late May or early June.

Some texts and specialists report that the Pacific Northwest has two subspecies of elk, the Rocky Mountain and the Roosevelt (or Olympic) elk. Others argue that though the two types exhibit slight physical differences due to their habitats (inland vs. coastal mountains), they are not true subspecies. Nearly all agree that using the Shawnee term "wapiti" would clear up international confusion. (An "elk" to Europeans is the animal we Americans call "moose.")

But most people who happen to spot a wild elk aren't concerned with those details. We go to the mountains and into the woods for other reasons. In the wilds, we receive many gifts—most of them intangible, like joy and serenity. But every so often, a gift received is as solid as an elk's antler that you can hold in your hand.

Pocket Gophers

Latin name: *Thomomys* spp.

Description: 8 to 12 inches long, depending on species; fur color variable, black and gray through brown and whitish; large claws on forepaws; long incisors always visible; small eyes and ears.

Habitat: Meadows and other open spaces.

Imagine you're a gopher, digging your way through the earth, when you come upon a particularly succulent root. You're not hungry, so you'd like to take it back to one of your storage rooms—but you can't carry it in your paws or your teeth because you need those for digging. What to do? You put it in a pocket, of course.

Pocket gophers are named for their two external, fur-lined pouches, which open at their cheeks and extend all the way down to their shoulders. They don't cram food into their mouth to transport it—they slip it into these outside pockets, just as we put things in the pockets of our jackets or jeans.

There are several species of pocket gophers in the Northwest, and they share certain characteristics useful for underground living. For example, they have powerful forelimbs—pocket gophers are downright beefy, as rodents go. Their front paws are equipped with five daggerlike claws designed for digging. The eyes and ears are small, since they are not especially useful below ground, but the facial whiskers and sparse hairs on the tail are extremely sensitive and help guide the animal through dark tunnels.

The tail is such an effective tactile instrument that the pocket gopher can run backward through its tunnels nearly as fast as it runs forward. In addition to cutting through roots, the large orange-brown front teeth also chomp through dirt, if needed, and loosen rocks. (Dirt doesn't get inside the rodent's mouth because the lips close neatly behind the teeth.) This constant use wears down the incisors, but, like those of all rodents, they continue to grow throughout the animal's life. The top teeth reportedly grow as much as fifteen inches in a year, the bottom ones nine inches.

Pocket gophers put all that equipment to use building extensive tunnel systems. They dig runways close to the surface, where they forage for edible plants. Food storage rooms and sleeping chambers are dug deeper down. Gophers also dig separate toilet rooms, closing them off once they are full. A gopher's entire tunnel system may be continuously rearranged, as various chambers and runways are closed off and new ones created.

Winter in the mountains doesn't stop a gopher's activities; it simply moves up into the snow and continues excavations there. The animals usually line their snow tunnels with dirt. With the spring thaw, the thin dirt tubes are gradually lowered to the ground, and once the snow has completely melted, these cores reveal the patterns and directions of the gopher's winter tunnels.

posed
teeth

External
Pocket
goes from
mouth to shoulder

They don't last long, however, crumbling and dissolving as they dry out.

With spring, the antisocial gopher's thoughts turn to procreation. The male ventures out of his tunnels to seek a mate, who tolerates him long enough to become pregnant. After a short gestation, five to six young are born in a grass-lined chamber. Shortly after weaning, the youngsters make their first appearance above ground in a nighttime scramble to dig a new home and begin their own solitary lives.

We tend to think of gophers as destructive: they certainly wreak havoc in our gardens and lawns. But their activities are inadvertently beneficial to soil and plants. Fecal pellets and forgotten food chambers add nutrients to soil. The animals' constant tunneling aerates the soil, encouraging plant growth and reducing rapid water runoff. It's estimated that a single gopher brings two and a quarter tons of soil to the surface each year. This soil-churning mixes subsoil with topsoil—a process that proved extremely valuable in the area around Mount St. Helens after its 1980 eruption.

Northern pocket gophers (*T. talpoides*), tucked safely underground, survived the massive eruption and proceeded with life as they always had. They excavated tons of soil from below ground, mixing it with the ash above ground. Plant seeds that landed in the gopher mounds were able to take root and grow, creating toeholds of green life in an ashen gray land. These green islands spread and, despite initial scientific predictions that nothing would grow in the area around the volcano for a hundred years, new plants appeared that same spring—thanks in part to the lowly, much-maligned pocket gopher.

Common Raven

Latin name: *Corvus corax*

Description: To 26 inches long; glossy black feathers with purple and green iridescence; long, pointed throat feathers create a shaggy ruff; thick black bill.

Habitat: Open areas in the mountains, clearings, roadways, above timberline.

As my car rounded a curve on a mountain road, I could see two all-black birds ahead, dining on roadkill at the side of the asphalt. I automatically assumed they were crows, but as the car neared, those birds loomed too large for mere crows. As they rose into the air on wings that spanned four feet, with shaggy throat feathers ruffling in the wind, and uttering harsh *krok*s at the interruption, I knew I should have recognized them sooner: I was in raven country now.

You can find ravens all the way down to sea level, but you're more likely to see them in the mountains—their smaller cousins, the crows, better fit the role of lowlanders, city-slickers, and suburbanites. Both ravens and crows are frequently described as brash and clever, and occasionally, even as having a sense of humor. A typical story from Canada describes ravens biding their time on a sloping, metal roof until someone walks past, whereupon the birds loosen clumps of snow that skid off the roof and onto the unsuspecting passerby's head. Likewise, an ornithologist once watched four ravens repeatedly slide down a snow bank on their tucked tails, apparently just for the fun of it.

The raven's intelligence is arguably the most highly developed of all birds. In a scientific test, a raven was given the task of retrieving a piece of food hanging from a long string beneath its perch pole. The bird reached down and grabbed a length of the string in its beak, secured this bit against the perch with a foot and again reached down to reel in more line, repeating the action until it had the treat in beak. Another raven observed the first, and then bested its technique: Picking up the string and holding it loosely in its beak, the second raven walked the length of the perch, which resulted in the string being pulled through its beak as it marched. The bird quickly came to the end of the string and claimed its prize.

In the wild, these birds use the same cunning to find food. They've been known to track a human, waiting for the moment to help themselves when the backpacker's meal is unattended, or the fisherman cleans a trout, or the hunter guts a deer. Ravens also keep an eye on roads, which they seem to regard as banquet tables serving entrees of roadkill. Although quick to claim new additions to the asphalt smorgasbord, they rarely become roadkill themselves. In addition to carrion, ravens enjoy fruit, grain, bird nestlings, eggs, reptiles, insects, amphibians, and small mammals.

It's likely that ravens mate for life, raising brood after brood together. During courtship, the male shows off his barrel rolls, swoops, and plummets. The pair makes tightly synchronized and coordinated "unison flights," and also soars together, male above the female, circling their nesting area. They may have two or more nests near the top center of evergreens, and annually rotate their use. Ravens add more stout sticks each year they use a nest, breaking these off trees rather than picking them up from the ground. The nest is made softer and warmer with a lining of hair or fur from carcasses, shredded bark, and moss. The female incubates four to six eggs while the male feeds her. Their young become independent in about a month and a half, but often remain with the parents in a family group throughout the winter.

Ravens have long enjoyed a featured role in human stories. For thousands of years, the Native peoples of the Northwest coast have known Raven as both Creator and Trickster. The Raven of legend might be noble or selfish, wise or foolish. He might be helpful, bringing fire to the People, or lusty, seducing women while their men are away. In many stories, he helps create the People and the Animals; in others, he is their sole creator. In addition to Indian legends, ravens are featured in ancient tales from Europe, the Far East, and the Middle East. They are found in the Bible and the works of Shakespeare, Dante, Charles Dickens, and Edgar Allen Poe. It's just probable that worldwide no bird has played a greater role in the lives and imaginations of humans than has the clever raven.

Black Bear

Latin name: *Ursus americanus*

Description: About 5 to 6 feet from nose to end of small tail; fur usually black but can be brown or reddish, often with white spot or markings on chest below neck; muzzle often lighter color than body fur; thick limbs.

Habitat: Usually forested areas, but sometimes forages in clearcuts.

Black bears are like bees; if you don't bother them, they're unlikely to bother you. The bears that approach campsites are those who have learned that people tend to bring food into the woods—and even these can often be driven away by pot-banging and hullabaloo of the type that bear visits naturally inspire. (Whether in the backcountry or at a developed campsite, campers should *always* store their food so bears cannot get at it. Nuisance bears, a danger to themselves and to us, result from our failure to do so.) Any type of bear should be considered potentially dangerous, but black bears usually go out of their way to avoid humans.

They also tend to avoid each other, unless it is mating season. In early and mid-summer, bears go courting. Males, called boars, advertise their availability at "bear trees" within their territory. Reaching up to their full height, they rake their claws down the trunk and may bite at it. A boar keeps informed of the status of the various females whose ranges overlap his via the scent of their urine and the odor they give off when in estrus. When he tracks down a receptive female, or sow, copulation lasts from ten to thirty minutes and may be repeated several times. The act of mating itself stimulates the release of eggs within the sow. Both males and females are likely to have more than one partner during the season, so the sow's cubs may have different fathers.

The sow's fertilized eggs, unlike those of many other mammals, do not immediately attach themselves to the uterus wall and begin growing. Instead, after dividing a few times, the eggs float freely within the uterus for the next few months. If the sow is unable to put on enough fat before hibernation to allow her to give birth to healthy cubs and feed them over the winter, her system will simply reabsorb the eggs.

Delayed implantation allows the cubs to be born during hibernation, in late winter. This improves the odds that by the following winter they will be big enough to have accumulated enough of their own fat reserves to survive their first full hibernation. Delayed implantation also allows the adult bears to concentrate on chowing down during the last critical weeks before hibernation instead of attending to the distractions of mating.

And chow down they do. With autumn comes the onset of a condition called *hyperphagia*, during which the bears seem insatiably hungry. In just two months a large boar may put on a whopping two hundred pounds. Bears are omnivorous, and they take advantage of berries, apples, and other fruits, fish, grains, green plants, insects and larvae, various mammals, and carrion.

When food supplies dwindle, it's time for bears to seek dens in which to spend the winter. A snug space is best to conserve body heat: a crevice between boulders, a hollow tree, or the space under the roots of an upturned tree. Once the site is chosen, the bear builds a cozy nest of grasses, leaves, bark, or needles, curls up on it, and usually stays put until spring. Unlike other hibernators, bears don't eat, urinate, or defecate during this time. Somehow bruins turn their urea, usually passed out of the body in urine, into protein. The new protein goes into muscle growth, so bears don't experience muscle loss or atrophy during their long sleep. Calcium is also recycled; the animals suffer no loss of bone mass or strength. Scientists are working to understand these processes, hoping the knowledge might help prevent muscle loss in astronauts in space and treat kidney ailments or osteoporosis in people on earth.

During hibernation, sows wake to give birth, usually to two or three young. Each weighs a mere eight ounces to one pound. By the time they emerge from the den in spring, the cubs will weigh eight pounds, about the weight of a human newborn. They will stay with their mother for about seventeen months, spending a second winter's hibernation with her. But the following spring, the sow will be ready to mate again, and she or one of her suitors will run off the yearlings.

Although the young males may wander widely before finding suitable territory, the female yearlings tend to settle within their mother's home range. Presumably this inheritance along matriarchal lines allows sows to further help perpetuate their genes via accommodating their daughters while ensuring against inbreeding with sons or brothers.

A black bear inspired one of America's most enduring and endearing icons. In 1902, President Teddy Roosevelt refused to shoot a small bear chained to a tree. Soon afterward, toymakers created the first "teddy bears." Perhaps it's a lingering memory of childhood security that makes some people want to believe black bears are docile creatures that can be approached with impunity. It's important to maintain a healthy respect for all bears and a wide distance from them—no matter how close and cuddly we once were with our teddies.

Snags and Nurse Logs

An old-growth forest is decidedly untidy. Standing dead trees, killed by insect attack or disease or perhaps decapitated by the force of a storm, remain upright long decades after they've pushed the last sap through their veins or produced their last needle. Their fallen comrades, logs in various stages of decay, litter the ground. Some trees invariably topple into streams, impeding the water flow. For many years, people were convinced this was no way to run a forest.

Seeking to improve a system that had evolved over millions of years, forest managers and workers cut down dangerous dead trees, called snags. They burned rotting logs with the rest of the slash so that tree seedlings had room to grow. They hauled logs out of streams to aid salmon in their upstream journey and the resulting fry in their downstream trip. Once waste and fire hazard were removed, more orderly, regimented forests reigned.

All of this seemed like a good idea at the time. At least until the scientists started poking around, taking notes, counting species, and comparing areas. The ever-curious and clarifying eye of scientific study began to reveal the integral role of standing dead and downed trees in maintaining a forest's health.

Studies have counted scores of animals that depend on snags for food, shelter, or both. Pileated woodpeckers, nuthatches, and chickadees chip out nest sites in the relatively soft wood of snags. Once holes have been opened up, flying squirrels, bats, owls, Vaux's swifts, wood ducks, deer mice, and other creatures call them home. Birds of prey use snags as perches from which to hunt or rest, as do flycatchers, swallows, and blue-birds. One study revealed that seventy-nine species of birds and mammals benefited from using snags.

Nor is the tree's service finished after it has succumbed to gravity's influence and found rest on the forest floor. Different organisms take advantage of the log, depending on its state of decay. Wood-boring insects, fungi, and bacteria lead the way for centipedes, millipedes, salamanders, shrews, voles, slugs, and snails. Both the interior and exterior of the log are used, especially as the bark sloughs off and creates cover for small mammals. Large fallen trees also provide shelter and dens for larger animals, including foxes, skunks, and raccoons. Researchers have counted one hundred and thirty vertebrate species that make use of logs on the forest floor.

Pileated Woodpecker holes

Plants, too, such as mosses and ferns, find a home on fallen logs. Downed trees are particularly hospitable to tree seedlings, especially those of hemlock, and are often called "nurse logs" because they provide a fine nursery for young trees. Theories as to why this is so include ready access to the nurse log's stored water or nutrients, and the role of fungi within the log in reducing disease or binding with the seedlings' rootlets to promote growth. As it decays, a fallen tree gradually releases nutrients accumulated over its lifetime, and organisms that live in the log add to this supply. Each downed tree acts as a long, slow, gradual fertilizing system that ultimately becomes part of the forest soil.

Similarly, trees that fall into streams and other waterways also slowly leach their nutrients into the water, and host specific organisms such as midges, dragonflies, and craneflies. Different species might ingest the wood or the algae that grow on the log, or tunnel within it. And the importance of fallen trees to salmon is well documented. Logs and other woody debris create pools and eddies where salmon can rest in their journeys up- and downstream. Fallen trees provide hiding places from predators and spawning and rearing habitats for the fish. They also slow the river, helping to retain the fallen leaves that are a basis for the aquatic food chain. When the river does flood, the logs help provide sheltered eddies and side channels that act as refuges for stream inhabitants.

Recognition of the important roles of snags, nurse logs within the forest, and woody debris in streams has led to changes in how forests are managed. While cultivated woods cannot compare to the unruly complexity of old-growth areas, forest managers are learning how to apply aspects of the ancient forest to create healthier, more ecologically diverse managed forests.

Engraver Beetles

Latin name: *Scolytus* spp.
Description: ⅛ inch; cylindrical bodies; shiny black or brown; clubbed antennae.
Habitat: Growing layer of wood just under a tree's bark.

ngraver beetles are responsible for those scrawling tracks we see on the inside of fallen bark pieces and on the bare trunks of dead trees. The scribblings look something like runes—some kind of ancient text that tells a story. And so they are. Engraver beetles write their life histories on trees, and these autobiographies can be read by anyone who takes a little time to decipher them.

One beetle begins the story. This first scribe may be either male or female, depending on species. It lands on a suitable tree, pierces the bark, and creates a nuptial chamber between bark and trunk. Typically, it releases an alluring scent (a pheromone), which is picked up by chemical receptors in the antennae of the opposite sex of its species. The arriving potential mate chirps a high-pitched greeting by rubbing body parts, usually its wing covers, against its abdomen. The sound is like a password in that it has to be the correct one for the particular species waiting within before the visitor is allowed into the chamber.

Having demonstrated by scent and sound that they are the same species

galleries in bark

of bark beetle, the two soon consummate the relationship. Now the female begins the first chapter of the family story. She munches a tunnel through the wood, laying her eggs at certain intervals along either side of it as she goes. Each egg is deposited in its own small niche. The eggs hatch into pale, legless, large-headed, hunched larvae that only a mother could love— except that even she doesn't, having left the tree, as did their father.

The larvae set to work on the next chapter of the family saga. Each chews its way along its own path, avoiding the nearby tunneling of its siblings. As the larva grows, its excavations widen accordingly. Eventually it is ready to pupate. It hollows out a slightly bigger space for itself and then ceases activity as it transforms into an adult beetle.

This accomplished, the new adult bores out through the tree's bark and flies off in search of an appropriate tree in which to write its final chapter— to which its children will add their own stories. By peeling bark off dead trees, or examining already denuded trunks or their fallen bark, you can read these family diaries. You will be able to recognize the straight-line engraving of the parent and perhaps even a wider circle located somewhere on its length that served as the nuptial chamber. (Some species, however, mate outside the tree on the bark.) The tunnels branching from this line are the work of the many children. The gradual widening of each tunnel reveals the growth of the larva that it held, and the bulbous ending marks where the larva pupated before leaving home.

Some scientists and interested amateurs can read even more. Each beetle species creates its own characteristic signature, which can actually be used to identify the species. There are many variations on the basic theme. The adult or the young may always tunnel with the wood's grain, may always tunnel against it, or may pay no heed to the grain. Eggs might be laid opposite one another or in an alternating pattern. The young might engrave straight lines, or ones that curve a certain way, or randomly meandering ones. Further, each beetle species is particular to certain species of trees and sometimes even to specific parts of those trees, perhaps a limb of a certain size.

Engraver beetles of the genus *Scolytus* generally do not harm healthy trees, although they do hasten the death of unhealthy or already-dying individuals. Some other members of the bark beetle family, however, can kill even healthy trees. The pine beetles (*Dendroctonus* spp.) have inflicted much damage, especially in some areas east of the Cascades, where years of fire suppression have led to epidemic numbers of beetles.

All the beetles of this family are quite small, and are rarely seen because they spend most of their lives hidden within trees. You may never have seen one of these ubiquitous forest dwellers, but you've no doubt seen evidence of the bark beetle's passage.

Huckleberries

Latin name: *Vaccinium membranaceum*

Description: 2 to 6 feet; leaves more or less oval; small, pink
bell-shaped flowers; berries dark blue to black.

Habitat: Forests, fire-cleared land, open huckleberry fields.

The seasonal pull of huckleberries is strong. By late August every
year, some Northwest residents find the lure irresistible, and berry
fields become feasting fields for bear, bird, and human alike.

A dozen species of huckleberries grow in the Northwest, and they are
traditionally important in the diet of many Northwest tribes. The species
favored in southern Washington and northern Oregon is *V. membranaceum*,
known by various common names, including thinleaf, mountain, and
black huckleberry. This species yields abundant, sweet, nearly black berries,
and forms acres of wild berry fields.

Gathering the berries was a part of the seasonal round practiced by various Indian tribes, including the Warm Springs and Wascos, who traveled
an annual pattern throughout the year, following the cyclical abundance of
their foods: roots, salmon, game, and berries. During late summer and fall,
they moved to the Cascades to take advantage of the bounty there.

Like the famous feasts that welcomed returning salmon, festivals of
thanksgiving marked the beginning of berry season. The gathered berries
were eaten fresh and were dried for later use by spreading huge quantities
of them alongside fires built in trenches. The women stirred the berries
with long wooden paddles to help them dry evenly. Not only were the
dried berries an important and nutritionally valuable food for the tribes

during the winter months, they were also an important trade item.

Because trees eventually overtake berry fields, the Indians used fire to maintain extensive berry fields. Winter rains would usually douse the fires, but if these were late, certain chosen tribal members were prepared to call upon the rains.

Berries and the religious rituals surrounding their gathering are still an important part of life to tribes such as the Warm Springs and Wascos. A handshake agreement in 1932 between a Yakama chief and a supervisor of what later became the Gifford Pinchot National Forest still preserves specific fields for Indian use. But because the Forest Service practiced strict fire suppression for many years, the berry fields have shrunk in acreage. In recent years, the Forest Service and the tribes have worked together to preserve the fields. Various management techniques are being explored, including the use of fire.

Birds, bears, and other animals do their part to perpetuate huckleberries by spreading the seeds far and wide in their droppings. Small bees are probably the most responsible for the inadvertent pollination of the plant's flowers. After a flower is fertilized, a growing berry soon replaces it. The withered fragments at the berry's end are the remnants of its flower.

Some naturalists get involved in discussions over whether these plants should properly be called huckleberries, blueberries, bilberries, or whortleberries. But I don't care what you call them as long as, come August, I get my share.

fireweed

Latin name: *Epilobium angustifolium*

Description: 3 to 8 feet; flowers usually rose-colored; numerous thin willowlike leaves.

Habitat: Disturbed areas, especially burned land, also clearings, meadows, fields, avalanche paths, along trails and open river banks.

When I first began working at Mount St. Helens National Volcanic Monument in 1985—just five years after that volcano's famous eruption—I was astounded by thousands of what looked like billowing snowflakes in the heat of summer. The flakes were really the downy white seeds of the fireweed, and there was a good reason why they were so numerous at Mount St. Helens.

Fireweed is a "pioneer species," meaning that it is one of the first plants to come in after a disturbance and paves the way for others. It especially thrives after a burn, as its name indicates, but fireweed is also one of the first settlers in areas that have been cleared by bulldozer or avalanche—or volcanic eruption.

As I explained this to one group of visitors at Mount St. Helens, a man told me he associated the plant with his military days in World War II. Stationed in London after it had been bombed and burned, he saw acres and acres of land covered by blooming fireweed. He recalled it as a lovely brightness in the aftermath of war.

In England, the plant is called "willow herb" because its eight-inch leaves are so similar to those of a willow tree. The dried leaves—rich in vitamin C—were often used in teas. And tea is not the only refreshment derived from fireweed. The plant's new shoots can be gathered and cooked like asparagus in the spring. Deer and elk also like to graze the plants. And beekeepers frequently transport their beehives to newly logged and burned areas; bees make a luscious, fragrant premium honey from fireweed.

Some Native American tribes also found fireweed useful. The Haida made a twine from the stem fibers, after drying and then soaking them. The cords were twisted or spun and used primarily for fishing nets. Other tribes added the seed fluff when padding mattresses and weaving blankets.

One reason fireweed does so well in open spaces is that it demands full sun. Once other species start growing around it, fireweed is eventually shaded out. Perhaps for this reason, the plant has two methods of reproducing itself. Rhizomes, or underground stems, produce buds, and this works well once the plant has already become established. But to get to those far-flung burned areas, a plant must rely on wind-borne seeds, which fireweed produces in abundance.

In the summer, each plant displays buds, flowers, and seedpods simultaneously. Fireweed opens its flowers successively, starting at the bottom. Once these first, lower flowers have been pollinated, perhaps by bees eager to make honey, the blooms develop into long, slender seed cases. Meanwhile, the upper flowers continue to open successively and be pollinated. The seed cases eventually dry and split open lengthwise into four thin strips that curl backward, releasing thousands of seeds launched on silky white tufts. Some naturalists have compared the plant's pink flower plumes to flames and its seeds to "smoke after the fire."

Despite fireweed's strong connection to forest fires and after-logging burns, the World War II veteran I met at Mount St. Helens will always associate the plant with a bombed-out Europe. And I'll forever remember the graceful lines and startling pink of fireweed in the midst of gray volcanic ash—and the snowy whiteness of its seeds in the middle of summer.

Spotted Owl

Latin name: *Strix occidentalis*
Description: To 19 inches; dark brown plumage with white spots on back, white horizontal splotches or spots on breast; eyes dark (no yellow pigment).
Habitat: Conifer forests with large, tall trees.

Late one night as we returned to our Forest Service housing, the headlights of my future husband's truck illuminated a small bundle on the road. Tim swerved around it and we pulled over to investigate. To our surprise, it was a dead spotted owl. Like many good naturalists who find an interesting dead animal, we took it home and put it in the freezer. Like bad naturalists, we didn't report our find immediately. This did not please the Forest Service wildlife biologist, who became aware of our discovery through roundabout means. After delivering a stern lecture about the penalties associated with harboring both a raptor and a threatened species (dead or alive), she confiscated our owl. We never saw Spotty again.

But Tim and I have since had the fortune of finding live spotted owls in old-growth forests. Those spots help them blend into the background so that it's easy to walk past one without ever seeing it. Perhaps because they rely so heavily on their camouflage, they are amazingly tame (some would say stupid) birds that allow close approach. Spotted owls also often respond—and sometimes even come—when you imitate their call.

A spotted owl uses that call to find a mate. A pair mates for life, and repeatedly uses the same nesting site—usually a hole in a tree, but occasionally an abandoned hawk's nest. The female incubates the two eggs she typically produces, while the male brings her food. He continues to be the family's sole provider for the first two weeks after the owlets hatch, and then the female helps meet the demands of their growing young. The owlets are fed ripped-up portions of the adults' fare—in our region, mostly flying squirrels and voles.

A young spotted owl may leave its nest before it is quite ready to fly. Sometimes the owlet lands safely on the forest floor and the parents are able to feed it there and protect it until it can fend for itself. Other times, the fall kills it (the nest may be as high as 200 feet above the ground), or it is snatched up by a predator such as a great horned owl.

The survival rate of spotted owls to breeding age (three years old) is very low. And the mated pairs produce young on average only every other year. Add to these factors the owls' need for large hunting territories within forests of large, tall trees, and the result is a species that has come to embody the conflict between preservation and cutting of old-growth forests. Throughout the 1980s and '90s, the spotted owl was a focal point as environmentalists sought to clarify the importance of an entire ecosystem and timber workers fought to save both their livelihood and their way of life.

In addition to the spotted owl's well-publicized woes, an additional threat has more recently been recognized. For reasons that are still under debate, barred owls (S. varia) have spread across the continent from the East and are now increasing in population on the West Coast. The barred owl is much more of a generalist in both its food and habitat requirements than the closely related spotted owl. Although the species are able to interbreed when their territories overlap, creating "sparred" offspring, it is far more likely that the barred owl will outcompete (and perhaps even prey upon) the spotted owl. In addition to being slightly larger, the barred owl is simply more aggressive than its relative; in territorial disputes, the barred wins. Some biologists hold out hope that the two species can coexist if given enough time and enough territory.

Nearly fifteen years after Tim and I found the dead spotted owl, I happened to see another owl land in a tree near that same road. I grabbed my binoculars and peered through the increasing dusk, hoping to make an identification of another spotty. But brown streaky spots on a lighter breast (rather than white spots on a darker background) revealed a barred owl instead of a spotted. Getting an uncommonly good look at such an evasive, nocturnal animal as an owl should have pleased me more. But that night the barred owl's proximity to an area I knew had harbored spotted owls simply seemed ominous.

American Dipper

Latin name: *Cinclus mexicanus*

Description: To about 8 inches long; males and females similar; body slate gray; short wings and tail; white ring around eye; yellow legs.

Habitat: Fast-moving mountain rivers; also occasionally lakes, ponds, and rushing streams from high elevations down to sea level.

The oddest thing about the American dipper, considering its food preferences, may be its feet. It would be reasonable to expect a bird that subsists on water insects and their larvae to have webbed feet, like a duck. But the dipper is a songbird. Like robins, chickadees, and wrens, it has the same unwebbed three toes forward and one behind.

Not that this seems to pose a problem for the dipper. Its strong feet grip the slippery stream bottom and allow it to walk about, completely submerged, prying larvae off underwater rocks. But the dipper does have other superb adaptations that allow it to go where no other songbird can. Its very dense plumage insulates it from the numbing cold of mountain streams, and an oil gland ten times larger than that of other songbirds allows a preening dipper to thoroughly waterproof its feathers. Like some water birds, the dipper has a flap over its nostrils that clamps shut to keep out water, and a white membrane that pulls up over the eye when needed to protect it from underwater detritus or waterfall spray.

Dippers are often found next to waterfalls. When leading visitors on summer hikes to a cooling waterfall in the Columbia River Gorge National Scenic Area, I always listened for the bubbling song of the dipper as we walked. Even as we neared the clamor of the falls, the bird's song was so loud it could be heard over the rush of water. Because its gray plumage tends to blend in with the rocks, the dipper's ringing call was often the first hint that it was in the area. Or sometimes the bird's peculiar bobbing would catch my eye. Dippers probably got their name not because they dip in and out of water but because, as they stand on rocks midstream or along the water's edge, they constantly bob up and down—about forty to sixty times a minute.

Once we'd spotted the bird, we'd watch for feeding activity or signs of nesting. A dipper sometimes walks through shallow water with just its head submerged, snapping up water beetles and the larvae of mosquitoes or caddisflies. It may also swim on the surface, but paddling with its songbird feet makes it a more awkward and less effective swimmer than a duck would be. Dippers often dive below the surface (as deep as twenty feet) and use their wings to "fly" underwater, rather than walking along the stream bottom.

When the bird flies in the air, it almost always follows the path of the river, staying a few feet above the water surface. Dippers are rarely seen flying over dry land. They are solitary birds that defend their stretch of waterway from other dippers—until breeding time.

To win a female, the male sings and struts before her, stretching his neck and partly spreading his wings. Occasionally, she might join in the performance, which concludes when they leap up together with breasts touching. Dippers build charming nests of mosses, about one foot in diameter, that are kept green by their proximity to the rushing stream. The nest may be situated on a rock in midstream, wedged in a crevice or on a ledge, or even placed behind a waterfall, so that the birds plunge through the pouring water to reach it. The female usually lays four to five eggs, and both parents bring insects and their larvae to the hatched young. If the male's territory is rich enough in food resources, he may have more than one mate.

The dipper is still sometimes called the water ouzel, as it was back in John Muir's day. The bird was one of the great naturalist's favorites. In his 1894 book *The Mountains of California*, Muir called it ". . . the mountain stream's own darling, the hummingbird of blooming waters." The American dipper is one songbird you won't find at your backyard bird feeder. Instead, look and listen for the darling whenever you find yourself beside rushing, falling, boiling, blooming water.

Lupines

Latin names: *Lupinus latifolius* (broadleaf lupine); *L. lepidis lobbii* (also known as *L. sellulus* or *L. lyallii*) (dwarf or alpine lupine)

Description: To 3 feet tall, depending on species; many pealike blue to purplish flowers; lobed leaves located near the base of stems; hairy seed pods.

Habitat: Open areas, including meadows and rocky slopes, at middle and high elevations, depending on species.

You may have noticed a family resemblance between the flowers of lupine and those of garden peas. As a member of the pea family, lupine shares with its relatives their ability to "fix" nitrogen. That is, these plants transform nitrogen from the air into a usable form, the surplus of which is released into the soil, thus enriching it and giving other plants access to nitrogen. Whenever I consider lupine's ability to fix nitrogen, I try to resist the thought of desperate plants and soil pleading, "Hey, Lupine—I need a fix! Can ya get me a fix?" The image of dirt and vegetation mainlining what lupine provides is not only unsavory and botanically incorrect, it is (horrors!) anthropomorphic.

It would also be anthropomorphic to call the lupine clever in the way it invites pollination. Each flower follows the familiar pea-plant design: five petals enclose ten stamens (pollen-covered male parts) and a single pistil (the female organ that receives pollen). The wide top petal of the flower is marked with two white spots called nectar guides, which flag down passing pollinators, particularly bumblebees. The insect, intent on gathering foodstuff, steps onto the flower's two lower, fused petals. Its weight depresses these petals, releasing the spring-loaded reproductive parts, which pop up to smack the insect's fuzzy abdomen. The female organ receives pollen—often that which was deposited by a flower the bee visited previously—while the male organs deposit their load, ready for the next flower the bee bumbles into.

As the flower ages, its nectar guides change from white to deep red. By the time this occurs, the flower's nectar is likely depleted, so the bees learn to spend their time on younger, more plunderable blossoms. Meanwhile, the fertilization of each flower leads to development of a seedpod. The pod dries and eventually splits open, catapulting its seeds. If the gymnastic seeds happen to land in a viable spot, they will germinate and send down a long water-seeking taproot. Lupine's abilities to find water and fix nitrogen make it an excellent pioneer plant. By homesteading on barren soil, it makes an area hospitable for later arrivals.

Lupine was one of the first plants to take root in Mount St. Helens' ash-covered landscape after the 1980 eruption. Scientists were not surprised that broadleaf lupine made an appearance in mid-elevation areas, but they were surprised to find dwarf, or alpine, lupine living below its usual high-elevation range. During the eruption, dwarf lupine plants rafted down from their lofty positions on a monstrously huge mudflow. The plants were able to establish themselves at lower elevations because the conditions there were so changed by the eruption. The forest had been swept away and the ground inundated with mud and ash, so that the landscape resembled an alpine one in its paucity of nutrients and in the harshness of temperature extremes. Dwarf lupine felt right at home.

The silver hairs on the leaves of this diminutive species help to reflect light and prevent desiccation. And the classic palmate shape of the leaves on any lupine species (like the spread-out fingers of a hand) seems to funnel rainwater directly down the stems toward the plant's roots. Or at least, so I would assume, based on the beguiling sight lupine offers after a rain or in the early morning. Each lupine leaf cups at its apex a remnant of rain or dew in such a way that the drop resembles a diamond. In addition to its valuable ability to alter nitrogen, lupine also transforms dewdrops and raindrops into sparkling gems.

Weasels

Latin names: *Mustela frenata* (long-tailed weasel); *M. erminea* (short-tailed weasel)

Description: Long-tailed: body to about 11 inches, and tail to 6¹⁄₂ inches; short-tailed: body to about 8 inches, and tail to 3¹⁄₂ inches. Cylindrical body, brown above and white or cream to yellow-orange below in summer; completely white in winter, except for tip of tail, which is always black.

Habitat: Brushy areas, edges of forests, usually near water; long-tailed also found in open areas.

The adjective used repeatedly in descriptions of this little carnivore is "ferocious." Although the weasel is only doing its job of staying alive, some of its habits are chilling to human sensibilities. Baby weasels have been known to turn on their littermates and devour them. Adults go on "killing sprees" during which they kill far more than they can eat. And weasels tend to appropriate a burrow by eating the current occupant—and then they line their new home with the fur plucked from its body.

In their defense, it should be said that weasels usually cache the extra food for later consumption, and we can assume that their victim's fur serves as comfy insulation rather than as some ghoulish trophy. Because the weasel often carries its prey back home to eat and adds the newly plucked fur to the walls of its home, it would seem that the nest would become smaller and smaller. But when the weasel presses the fur into place, it simultaneously pushes the walls a bit farther out. The longer the animal occupies the same nest, the roomier and warmer it becomes.

Warmth is important to an animal built like the weasel. Its long, thin body readily dissipates heat, and its high metabolism demands a lot of food for fuel. Not surprisingly, the weasel is a consummate hunter. A weasel on the prowl is impressive in its audacity, intensity, and thoroughness. It investigates every nook and crevice, zigzagging throughout its territory, poking into holes and diving into underground burrows. A weasel feeds mostly on the smaller, ground-dwelling mammals: chipmunks, ground squirrels, moles, pocket gophers, pikas, shrews, rats, and mice. On occasion, it also feeds on birds, fish, frogs, earthworms, and some insects. More impressively, it will attack and kill prey larger than itself, such as rabbits. The long-tailed weasel also goes after mountain beavers ("boomers").

The mountain-dwelling individuals of both species turn white in the winter to better blend in with the snow, while those at the lower, soggier elevations remain brown all year. Furriers call both species of white-coated animal "ermine" once they have been turned into coats, but naturalists tend to call only the short-tailed weasel by the name "ermine" or "stoat."

The two species have the same reproductive strategy. For a period in the summer months, the normally solitary male and female weasels agree to spend a little time together. Long-taileds reportedly copulate for up to three hours. Although the young take only twenty-five to twenty-seven days to develop and be born, this does not take place until about seven or eight months after mating, due to a process called delayed implantation. The fertilized eggs stop developing and are not implanted in the uterus until the following year. After this occurs, the young are born in mid-April or mid-May.

The average litter consists of six or seven babies, which are finely covered with white hair. They remain in the nest until they are weaned, at which time the mother begins to bring them meat, and soon they tag along on her hunting trips to get an idea of how it's done. The young are probably on their own at about three to four months of age; by this time they are able to make their own kills.

A weasel pursues prey ruthlessly, leaps upon it, and drives its front teeth into the base of the victim's skull. Larger prey, such as a rabbit, is brought down by a bite to the throat. Once the weasel has clamped onto the killing spot, it does not let go until the victim has stopped struggling. One biologist has suggested that "if a weasel were as big as a cougar, no one would dare venture outside."

Bushy-Tailed Woodrat

Latin name: *Neotoma cinerea*

Description: Up to 28 inches including tail, which can be almost half the animal's length; gray to black fur above, whitish below, including tail and feet; tail and ears also furry.

Habitat: Cliff and rock-slide areas, rocky outcroppings, and conifer forests, as well as abandoned cabins and other human structures.

Woodrats deserve a better name. Their reputation is sullied because people tend to associate them with the offensive, introduced Norway rat, which is much more likely to invade residences. In the mountains, the only kind of house a bushy-tailed woodrat moves into is an abandoned cabin in the woods. (It's a different story along the coast, where a paucity of suitable habitat sometimes leads woodrats to take up residence in houses already quite occupied by humans.) Bushy-tails also live in old mine shafts, woodsheds, rocky crevices, and hollow trees. In all of these places they make a cozy, cuplike nest, usually out of soft materials.

Once its domicile is established, a woodrat's thoughts turn to interior design. For reasons known only to themselves, woodrats like to take home little souvenirs of their nocturnal travels, a habit that has earned them the name "packrats." Bones, pieces of dried dung, and string will do, but shiny, metallic objects such as gum wrappers, coins, and bottle caps are especially prized. When the items taken are forks or spoons or watches, woodrats can become a

front

hind

nuisance to backpackers and campers. Packrats are also called traderats because if one is already carrying a stick or stone when it comes across a nice shiny ring or some other more intriguing tidbit, it will drop the first item in order to pick up the better one.

When they're out and about at night, bushy-tails are also searching for food. They eat flowers, seeds, stems, twigs, tree shoots, berries, and fungi. They'll also consume some insects and small amounts of carrion. During their rounds, woodrats must keep a watchful eye out for predators. Their many enemies include foxes, coyotes, owls, and large snakes. When they sense danger, rather than crying out, woodrats are more likely to drum their feet, which seems to act as a warning to other woodrats nearby.

Bushy-tails may produce two litters a year, with an average of two to four young in each. The blind, hairless babies immediately crawl up their mother's fur and latch onto a teat. There they remain for nearly three weeks until they are weaned, carried right along as their mother forages for food and trinkets. Should a predator disturb the nest while the family is in it, the mother can quickly escape with her firmly attached young.

The dusky-footed woodrat (*N. fuscipes*) is also found at lower elevations in western Oregon. In open areas, this woodrat builds a stick home that can reach an impressive eight feet high and eight feet in diameter. Chambers inside the lodge serve as maternity ward, storage rooms, toilets, and bedrooms. The chambers are interconnected with runways, some of which also lead to the outside. Along the coast, dusky-footed woodrats tend to build more discreet, well-hidden stick homes.

Bushy-tails, too, sometimes build stick homes, but these are less elaborate than those of the dusky-foots, up to only three feet in diameter and a few feet high. They tend to be built at ground level in hollow trees, but some have been found wedged up inside trees. Woodrats may also build stick nests on branches of trees, as high up as fifty feet.

But whether a home is big or small, high or low, belonging to a dusky-footed or a bushy-tailed, it is likely to be decorated with treasures the woodrat just couldn't resist. The animals' tendency to gather collectibles is so humanlike that it's endearing—as long as you're not on the receiving end of a woodrat's lopsided "trade."

Cougar

Latin name: *Puma concolor* (formerly *Felis concolor*)

Description: Up to 8 feet long from nose to tail tip; tawny or brownish overall; round ears with no tufts; thick, cylindrical tail about two-thirds the length of the body.

Habitat: Dense or open forests; meadows with sufficient cover.

We're more ambivalent now about cougars than we were a few decades back. It was easy to admire the big cats' wildness when field guides lamented that you were unlikely to ever see one of the "elusive creatures." It's more unsettling when newspaper articles shriek that people are increasingly being stalked and killed by the "stealthy top predators." Nobody wants to be prey.

Further disconcerting news: the place where a large number of attacks have occurred is the Pacific Northwest. There is much speculation over why Vancouver Island, B.C., is such a hot spot for cougar attacks. One theory is that a scarcity of available prey may entice the cougars toward settlements that host dogs, cats, and raccoons as well as humans. Various other theories suggest that the genetically isolated island population may have become more aggressive than other populations.

While it's true that attacks on humans have increased in many Western states (as a result of the animals' increasing numbers and suburban encroachment on their shrinking habitat), it's also true that such occurrences are still *extremely* rare. A person is more likely to die from a dog attack, bee sting, or bite from a black widow spider or rattlesnake.

The favorite prey of cougars (also commonly called mountain lions or pumas) is deer, not humans. The cats also take elk, rabbit, beaver, marmot, porcupine, small rodents, and other animals. A cougar usually stalks its intended victim, gradually and patiently closing the distance until it can pounce. If you've ever seen a house cat crouched belly-to-ground, alternately freezing and sneaking up on an unsuspecting bird or ball of yarn, you know how a cougar hunts.

Mountain lions kill by two methods. They either clamp onto an animal's throat and asphyxiate it, or bite the back of its neck to sever the spinal cord. Researchers speculate that cougars use their nerve-rich canine teeth and sensitive whiskers to locate the correct spot before plunging an inch-and-a-half-long tooth between the victim's vertebrae. Their remarkably raspy tongues later help to remove flesh from bone.

Cougars are loners except during mating season, when their mating caterwaul is said to resemble the blood-curdling scream of a woman in distress. Settlers believed the cry was a deliberate attempt to lure them into the woods so the waiting cat could kill them. But the animals' intentions are amorous rather than murderous; they may couple an impressive fifty to seventy times a day for at least three or four days.

Although cougars can breed at any time of year, most births occur between April and September. The female will raise the young alone. Two or three kittens, or cubs, are born in an average litter, each weighing about a pound. Unlike their parents, cougar kittens have dark spots on their coats, ringed tails, and startlingly blue eyes. By the time they are ready to strike out for their own territory at eighteen months to two years old, their coloration will have changed to match that of their parents—including their eyes, which will be a greenish yellow.

And, like their parents, each will be so extraordinarily elusive that few people will ever catch a glimpse of one. That said, it's always a good idea for people who spend time in the wild to have a little knowledge on their side.

In the unlikely event that you should notice a lurking mountain lion, immediately pick up any children, who are the most likely members of a group to be attacked. Look the cat directly in the eye, and maintain eye contact because the animal moves closer when its prey is not looking at it. Don't attempt to run from it. Raise your arms to look larger. If you can reach them without crouching or bending over, use sticks, rocks, or other weapons to drive off the cougar. If it attacks, fight back. Don't follow the well-known advice for grizzly attacks of playing dead; that works only because a grizzly is not usually interested in eating you, while an attacking cougar most certainly is.

But to *really* increase your odds of surviving into old age, consider posting a lightning rod everywhere you go—death by lightning is six hundred and fifty times more likely than death by cougar.

Mountain Goat

Latin name: *Oreamnos americanus*

Description: 5 to 5½ feet long; 3 to 3½ feet tall at shoulder; long white fur; bearded chin; shoulder hump; short tail; curved black horns.

Habitat: Alpine and subalpine cliffs and steep slopes in the Washington Cascade and Olympic Mountains.

Mountain goats live on the edge. As they perch on high peaks and alpine cliffs, the white of their shaggy coats matches the brilliant snow and contrasts with their black hooves, noses, and eyes. They are handsome, sure-footed animals that for many people epitomize the spirit of the mountains.

Several adaptations allow mountain goats to maintain their foothold on the Northwest's steepest and most rugged terrain. They have a sense of balance that a gymnast would envy. And, like the best gymnasts, they have relatively short legs and compact bodies, giving them a low center of gravity. The two toes of their hooves spread apart for better grip, and flexible pads on their soles add even more traction.

A heavy coat protects the animals from the chilly winds that blow through their alpine home. Underneath the furry outer coat is a layer of soft, thick wool that was prized by some Northwest Indian tribes, who spun it into yarn and wove the yarn into warm blankets.

The males' outer coats can become dingy—if not disgusting—in late fall, as they prepare for the rut, or mating. A billy seeks to impress the females (and other males with whom he is competing for the nannies' attention) by digging a hollow, into which he deposits urine and feces, and then wallowing in the mucky pit. The odor billies carry apparently telegraphs information about their health and makes it less likely that the males will have to duke it out to determine who is superior. Fights are rare, but can be deadly when they occur; the males slash at one another's flanks and bellies with their horns.

Months after the female has chosen her partner and mated, she gives birth to one, or occasionally two, young. The kids are able to stand and nurse within minutes of birth. After a few days, they can follow their mother nearly anywhere, but until that time, they "freeze" like fawns whenever she must leave them. Nannies and kids form nursery groups that travel and feed together, but for the rest of the year, mountain goats are more solitary, or may group in small bands of up to five animals.

Few predators can compete against the goats' agility on a cliff. A mountain lion may occasionally take an adult, but this is more likely to happen when the goat is feeding in a meadow. The kids are more at risk from predation by the big cats, and also from dive-bombing golden eagles, which topple the young off ledges to their deaths and then swoop down to eat at leisure. But avalanches, rockslides, starvation, disease, and the odd misstep that causes a fall are more likely to end a mountain goat's rock-climbing career.

This member of the antelope family (the mountain goat is neither goat nor sheep) is native to the Washington Cascades. Because they were wiped out in some areas of their range and have been reintroduced, some people erroneously believe they were not native to the state. It is true, however, that mountain goats are not native to the Olympics, and their introduction there has caused destruction of alpine meadows. As a result, Olympic National Park is removing all of its mountain goats, a process that will take many years. Mount St. Helens managed that same result in one day, when the eruption on May 18, 1980, killed its entire population of (introduced) mountain goats. Nothing yet has prepared these animals to counter explosive volcanic eruptions, but barring such events, mountain goats are superbly adapted to live on some of the most inhospitable and exciting terrain in the Pacific Northwest.

Pika

Latin name: *Ochotona princeps*

Description: About 5 to 6 inches long; brown coat; round ears with white margins; stubby, inconspicuous tail.

Habitat: Piles of rocks, including lava rock, usually at high elevations but sometimes at lower (such as the Columbia River Gorge); in the Cascades Range but not found in the Olympics or Coast Ranges.

Pikas spend the summer making hay while the sun shines. From early June through November, their rockpile community bustles as they race about, gathering grasses, laying them out in the sun to cure, and secreting them away in caches deep within the rocks. Although they live together in a colony, it's every pika for itself. They do not share dens or food supplies, so each is intent on putting in its own stash of food to last the long winter.

They do keep each other informed of the approach of potentially dangerous animals, however, which is why you're likely to hear a pika before you see one. The animal's warning *eenk* call is nasal and surprisingly loud. And it usually comes from a different direction than you think it does—pikas seem to throw their voices like ventriloquists. The easiest way to spot pikas once you've heard them is to scan the rockpile for movement. But since the little animals tend to freeze when they sense danger and blend in wondrously with the rocks, try looking for the one thing that is incongruous to the background: their cute little round, white-rimmed ears.

If you sit down and remain quiet, business in the colony will return to normal. You can watch individuals grooming and apparently snoozing in the sun, while others make a beeline from the relative safety of the rockpile to an adjacent meadow and back, pausing each way at specific spots to assess danger. An individual may make over a hundred trips a day to the meadow to feed. From June to November, a pika makes perhaps an additional two hundred daily trips to gather plants to dry. These it carries back crosswise in its mouth and arranges them just so to be cured in the sun and also to proclaim the animal's territory within the rocks.

A pika's busy itinerary is regularly interrupted by the need to chase other pikas out of its territory and to give and respond to alarm calls. A resounding *eenk* will warn others of predators like foxes, but should a weasel—a pika's worst enemy—begin scouting the rockpile, the little loudmouths shut right up. Slinky weasels can follow a pika down into its burrow, so it's best not to call attention to oneself.

Pikas resemble guinea pigs, but they're actually in the rabbit family. Like rabbits, the males have testes in front of their penises rather than behind, and they have eight incisor teeth rather than the four of rodents. The extra pairs of teeth, top and bottom, are much smaller than those of rodents and are located directly behind the large front incisors. But, like those of rodents, the pikas' front teeth continuously grow and are worn down by use.

Although not as prolific as rabbits, pikas are likely to have two or perhaps even three litters a year, with an average of three or four babies in each. By the time they are half grown, at about four weeks, the young are already making hay and claiming their own territories—usually toward the less-desirable center of the rockpile. Although it might seem that the center would be the safest area, the edges are best because their inhabitants are exposed and vulnerable for shorter periods than those living farther from the meadow grasses.

In addition to gathering hay, the pika has gathered a lot of common names. It's been called rock rabbit, whistling or piping hare, little chief hare, and coney or cony (originally an old European term for a species of rabbit). And should you discuss the matter with a biologist or a Canadian, you might find that they pronounce pika as "PEE-ka," though most of the rest of us say "PIE-ka." When in doubt, you can always fall back on the old standby of "little haymaker"—nobody will argue with that.

large, rounded ears
Dense coat for the cold
EEENK!
Front
Furry feet leave soft tracks
HIND

Snow and Avalanches

Although avalanches are often described as making a roaring sound, my friend Dan didn't hear anything when the lead person in his skiing party was swept away. Dan had been looking down at the ski tracks he was following, so he didn't see Joe consumed by the rush of snow either. He simply looked up, and his friend was gone.

Because the four backcountry skiers were aware that slides are a danger in undeveloped ski areas, they had spread out as they crossed the white expanse. Dan also carried an avalanche shovel. When the remaining three realized what had happened, Dan shucked his pack, grabbed the shovel, and raced down the lumpy spillway, looking for some sign of Joe. It wasn't until he was nearly to the end of the slide that he finally spotted his friend's red jacket sleeve poking up from the snow.

Joe had remembered to "swim" as the avalanche carried him and, as it stopped, to hold his arms in front of his face to create a air pocket. Despite his skis and heavy pack, he ended up near the surface, with a direct opening to air and his arm crooked out of the snow. Completely immobilized, Joe could feel his legs being twisted as the snow shifted and settled. He was solidly packed in and could not have gotten free without Dan's help.

In many cases, the potential for an avalanche can be recognized. It's imperative that anyone who travels in snowy, undeveloped areas take an avalanche safety course to learn to recognize that threat and to know, as Dan and Joe did, how to react should a slide occur.

Most avalanche victims trigger the slides that kill them, either by their weight or by vibrations from their movements. But avalanches can also be launched by a rapid, heavy snowfall adding its weight to an already-steep, less-dense snowpack. And fluctuating temperatures, especially common in the springtime, allow melted snow water to percolate down until it reaches a hard crust, where it acts as a lubricant to help propel a slide.

But the vast majority of us who venture into the white stuff find our experiences delightful or challenging rather than threatening. However, as any skier who has both glided over powder snow and trudged through moist "Cascade concrete" can attest, some kinds of snow are more fun than others. The difference begins with the snowflakes, which are actually collections of ice crystals. Scientists who study snowflakes call them "snow crystals" and divide them into seven types, based on their shapes. There are simple needlelike and columnlike shapes, but the type most people picture at the word "snowflake" is the stellar crystal. These are the classic Hallmark-card variety, six-armed, symmetrical, and intricate flakes.

The shape a snow crystal ultimately assumes depends on various factors, the most important of which is temperature. More elaborate crystals form at higher temperatures and simpler crystals at lower ones, although a single snowflake can be shaped by different temperatures as it moves through the atmosphere.

To begin with, a snowflake requires some kind of nucleus around which to form. This might be dust, sea salt, industrial pollution, volcanic ash, or any other microscopic bit of matter high in the atmosphere. Water vapor adheres to the particulate, freezing around it in a delicate hexagonal of ice. The ice crystal might rise in updrafts or fall toward earth, and as it does so, it encounters differing temperatures and amounts of water vapor that cause it to accumulate additional frozen crystals. The symmetrical, six-sided formation of the crystals follows the basic molecular pattern of water. When a snowflake is heavy enough, it falls to earth.

It is true that no two snowflakes are ever alike? The answer depends on how you define "snowflake." Certainly some of the smallest snow crystals, simple hexagons, show no obvious difference in their shapes. But when "snowflake" refers to the elaborate stellar flakes, the statement is most likely true. Individual flakes form around different nuclei and take different paths through the atmosphere, thereby encountering the different conditions that shape them. The staggering number of water molecules connected in a single flake (in the range of ten quintillion, or 10,000,000,000,000,000,000) and the different ways they can arrange themselves in three dimensions suggest that the number of shapes flakes can assume is incalculable. Snowflakes are apparently as unique as the individual people who ski, sled, or snowshoe through them.

Marmots

Latin name: *Marmota* spp.

Description: To about 30 inches long, including stubby tail; stout bodies; short legs and tails; small eyes and ears. Species differ in coloration of reddish or yellowish tones, and varying shades of brown or gray.

Habitat: Alpine meadows with well-drained soil, rocky outcroppings, rock slides.

C all them marmots, call them whistle-pigs or rockchucks—just don't call 'em late for dinner. Marmots spend long summer days feasting—transforming grasses and wildflowers into enough fat to sustain them through six or seven months of hibernation. By the time the vegetation dries out or the first frosts arrive, marmots are usually so fat their bellies drag on the ground.

In addition to the leafy parts of grasses and flowers, marmots also eat the roots and seeds. The animals themselves are typically eaten by coyotes, golden eagles, hawks, and foxes, with young ones being the most vulnerable to predation. Because marmots are fat, succulent animals not particularly fleet of foot, they obviously require some defensive strategy. They create it through their social structure. As any alpine hiker knows, marmot sentries stand alert while their fellows feed, and let loose piercing whistles should any other creature venture too near.

The marmot's "whistle" is actually a call or shriek because it's produced with the vocal cords. Different calls transmit corresponding levels of urgency: a person hiking on a well-traveled

FRONT

HIND

nearby trail won't inspire as mad a dash for safety as will a swooping golden eagle. Adults in a colony take turns at guard duty, usually on a prominent rock, sitting erect with their forepaws hanging down. In national parks, where they are protected, marmots become quite used to the presence of people, but even the wilder ones are likely to tolerate you if you sit quietly some distance away.

Some marmot species are relatively solitary; in other species, several dozen may live in a large colony. Those living in rocky outcroppings make their burrows in crevices, and those living in alpine meadows dig impressive underground burrow systems. There are usually several entrances, often located beneath rocks.

Marmots mate shortly after hibernation ends. A courting couple embrace and utter mewing calls to one another, or sometimes play a little

SILVERY
MUZZLE
& BACK

rough, grinding their teeth and shoving each other around as foreplay. After a gestation of five weeks, a mother marmot births two to nine young in a grass-lined burrow. The babies are born blind and naked. They stay safely below ground for more than a month, until they are ready to venture out of the burrow and begin chowing down like the adults.

But life for marmots isn't all eating and no play. The youngsters, and sometimes the adults, have rousing games that we would recognize as tag or hide-and-seek or wrestling. They also occasionally roll down slopes, but whether this is part of the fun or adolescent clumsiness has been debated. On warm summer days, they may take a break to spread out like furry rugs on rocks and soak up the rays.

Yellow-bellied marmots, living on the eastern slopes of the Cascades, begin their long sleep during the summer months. Summer slumber, called estivation, begins during the hot weather when the marmots' food supplies have dried up. With the coming of winter, estivation gives way to hibernation, so these animals stay below ground, or deep within rocky out-croppings, for more than half the year.

The more-alpine hoary and Olympic marmots stay active throughout the summer. But eventually they too go underground, plugging their entrance holes from the inside with dried grasses, dirt, and stones. An entire family, perhaps up to fifteen animals, will hibernate together. As they enter deep sleep, their oxygen use decreases and their body temperatures drop. Heartbeats slow from over one hundred per minute to a mere three or four. The end of hibernation depends on altitude: it generally occurs later in higher elevations. After many months, the marmots awaken, no doubt to growling tummies, and once again attend to the serious business of getting fat.

Volcanoes

Before Mount St. Helens' dramatic 1980 wake-up call, many Northwesterners were unaware that the Cascade Range's highest peaks were volcanoes. But the eruptive histories of these mountains were legendary among the local Indian tribes. The Klickitat, Cowlitz, and Coast Salish, for example, saw St. Helens, Mount Hood, and Mount Rainier involved in a fiery lovers' triangle that occasionally resulted in thrown boulders and flows of hot mud.

Geologists and volcanologists were also well aware of the peaks' volcanic status. The volcanoes throughout the Cascades, from Mount Garibaldi in southern British Columbia to Lassen Peak in Northern California, are all part of the "Ring of Fire." The evocative phrase describes the many active, dormant, and extinct volcanoes that encircle the Pacific Ocean, including those in South, Central, and North America, Japan, the Philippines, Indonesia, and New Zealand.

The Pacific Rim is a hotbed of volcanic (and earthquake) activity because the forces of plate tectonics are at work deep under the water and land. Like pieces of an ill-fitting, slowly shifting jigsaw puzzle, massive slabs of the Earth's crust known as plates jostle up against one another, with oceans and continents riding about on top of them. Plates under the Pacific Ocean are forced apart by upwelling lava, and pushed toward the plates carrying the continents. The plates meet one another in what has been described as a slow collision, and the heavier oceanic plate is subducted under the continental one. Underground chambers of magma develop from the resulting heat and pressure, fueling volcanic eruptions.

Our classic image of a volcano is one that spews great flowing fountains of molten rock, Hawaiian style. The volcanoes of Hawaii, called shield volcanoes because their broadly sloping sides resemble a warrior's shield lying down, are formed almost exclusively by such flows of lava. The Cascades commonly produce stratovolcanoes (also called composite volcanoes), which are high-sided and steep. These are built up by eruptions of molten lava alternated with eruptions that hurl rocks from the vent, launch ash, and/or spew pyroclastic flows (flows of hot—but not liquefied—rocks). Mount St. Helens' 1980 eruption included an explosive blast, a tremendous column of ash and pumice, and superheated flows of pumice that traveled down the mountain's flanks at up to eighty miles per hour.

Pumice is created when dissolved gases within the magma suddenly come out of solution during an eruption. In a glass of beer, gases that were dissolved in the liquid are released and create a foaming head; similarly, depressurized lava produces frothy pumice.

Our Cascades volcanoes are also noted for their mudflows, which St. Helens provided during its big eruption. Mudflows typically result from a mixing of melted snow and glacial water with ash, lava, or landslide debris. They are extremely thick and powerful flows that can be relatively fast moving. St. Helens' Toutle River mudflow ripped bridges from their moorings and was thick enough to raft not only boulders but also cars and even an abandoned logging truck still carrying its logs.

The threat of mudflows is perhaps the greatest danger of the Cascade volcanoes. The flows can develop without eruption activity where there are unstable slopes. Geologists point out that Mount Rainier is especially susceptible to mudflows and that it once launched one of the world's largest mudflows, which traveled all the way to Puget Sound. Today, communities such as Orting, Carbonado, and Greenwater, all relatively close to Rainier and all located in valleys that have had previous mudflows, are considered at risk.

The question "Will Mount Rainier, Mount St. Helens, or one of the other Cascade volcanoes erupt again?" is easily answered: Absolutely yes. The more difficult question to answer is "When?" Maybe not during your lifetime. But the Cascades have reliably produced, on the average, at least one major outburst per century. Since 1980, every Northwesterner has known that our postcard-pretty mountains are volcanoes—and they are certainly not extinct.

Pacific Silver fir

Latin name: *Abies amabilis*

Description: To 180 feet tall; remarkably straight, relatively slender trunks have smooth gray bark with white blotches (base of older trees can be scaly); dark-green needles lean toward growing tip, hiding the twig; two white lines on underside of each needle; barrel-shaped 3- to 5-inch-tall cones stand erect on upper branches.

Habitat: Coast range, Olympics, and west side of Cascades, generally from 2,000 to 5,000 feet.

Pacific silver firs are a patient sort of tree. They may spend many long years in the dense shade of a tall forest, accepting what little sunlight comes their way and waiting for their big chance. The opportunity that knocks down all the big trees may come in the form of an avalanche or a windstorm. In 1980, at Meta Lake, eight miles from Mount St. Helens, an eruption did the trick.

On May 18, hurricane-force winds swept the area, hammering down the tall western red-cedars, hemlocks, and Douglas-firs. Scientists who visited Meta Lake soon after the eruption declared that it would be a hundred years before any plant again raised its green head above the blanketing gray ash. But that was before the snow that lay under the ash began to melt, and before the little Pacific silver firs, bent over and buried by the snow—and therefore protected from the eruption blast—began to straighten up from beneath their load.

Because the area surrounding St. Helens was still snow-covered in May, many more small animals, trees, and other plants survived the eruption than had been imagined. Gradually the survivors emerged from the mono-chrome gray. The largest of the skinny little silver firs around Meta Lake

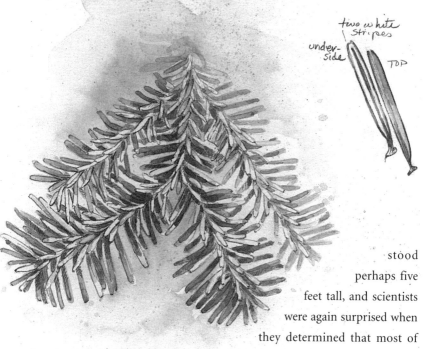

two white stripes

under-side

TOP

stood perhaps five feet tall, and scientists were again surprised when they determined that most of the trees were forty or fifty years old. The wizened trees' patience had paid off. Now that the sun-hogging big trees were out of the way, the little silver firs began stretching quickly upward, making up for lost time.

When I first began leading visitors to Meta Lake in 1985, I would pause beside a conveniently located silver fir near the beginning of the trail. While explaining how the trees had survived the eruption, I would grab the little fir's top, or leader, and bend the tree down to demonstrate. Within a year or two I could no longer reach the leader; in the years since, the tree has grown so much that it now towers over the trail. The last time I visited Meta Lake, I had to lean way back to see the whole tree.

David Douglas, perhaps the best known early naturalist to explore the Northwest, first encountered Pacific silver fir near Mount Hood in 1825. The scientific name he bestowed on it translates as "lovely fir." But by the late 1800s, there was some doubt in the scientific community as to whether the lovely fir actually existed. Delegations from England had failed to find it, and it was generally agreed that Douglas must have misidentified a grand fir (which itself had also been originally described and named by

Douglas). It wasn't until 1880 that three respected botanists "rediscovered" the mythical silver fir.

Grouse, Clark's nutcrackers, and Douglas squirrels (named after you-know-who) all eat the seeds from the tree's pudgy purplish cones. Come fall, hikers occasionally find themselves bombarded by the pitch-coated cones as the industrious squirrels clip them from branches high above. Although it can feel like a sneak aerial attack, the squirrels' intentions are (probably) benign. The animals later retrieve the harvested cones from the ground and stash them as winter food supply.

Pacific silver firs may have eluded the European scientific community for over fifty years, but Douglas squirrels and other inhabitants of the Pacific Northwest knew about them all along.

Tailed frog

Latin name: *Ascaphus truei*

Description: To 2 inches long; tan, olive, gray, or brown to nearly black, with dark blotches; small bumps on skin; vertical pupils; no external eardrum; males have short, soft "tail."

Habitat: Permanent, fast-moving, clear, cold streams, usually in forested areas; up to 7,000 feet.

When, in your rambles, you come across a cold, swift stream, it's worth taking a few minutes to hunt for tailed frogs. Even a small stream can harbor these elusive amphibians. Dip your fingers into the chill water to pick up and turn over rocks (after first noting how they lie so you'll be able to replace them exactly as you found them). Look closely: tailed frogs are small and blend in wonderfully with their environment.

You're much more likely to find the tadpoles than their secretive elders. These have the usual fat-bodied, slim-tailed polliwog shape, although they are relatively wide and flat. They are black, brown, or reddish brown and can usually be identified by a conspicuous white spot at the tip of the tail. Look for them clinging to the bottoms, or even the tops, of moss-free rocks. They attach themselves to cobbles (or, perhaps, your hand) with a wide, suction-cup mouth to avoid being washed downstream. The tadpoles vacuum their way over rocks, sucking up algae and diatoms as nourishment.

The young metamorphose slowly in the cold mountain streams and may remain tadpoles for up to five years, depending on the climate of their particular site. It takes another few years for the froglets to grow to sexual maturity. Adult females are slightly larger than males, and lack the "tail"

the species is named for, which is a good hint that this protuberance is not really a tail after all: this male frog is the only amphibian in the Northern Hemisphere that has an external copulatory organ.

A frog sporting something akin to a penis seems strange until you consider the habitat of the tailed frogs. You won't find them lazing about some sluggish backwater pond or lake. Sperm released over a cluster of eggs in the usual froggy fertilization method would be washed away in a rushing mountain stream.

Internal fertilization is not the only lifestyle difference found in tailed frogs. Perhaps because they would not be able to outcompete the singing of the stream, these frogs have no vocal sacs and do not sing to find a mate; correspondingly, they also lack eardrums (the round membranes on either side of the head, obvious in many frog species). Instead, males probably crawl along the bottom of streams in search of a partner.

Mating takes place in fall, but the female doesn't lay her eggs until early the following June or July. She attaches her eggs (usually about forty), linked like a beaded necklace, low on a rock or boulder. The hatchlings that emerge about six weeks later lack pigment and are initially transparent.

As adults, tailed frogs are nocturnal, which is one reason why we seldom encounter them. Under cover of darkness, they sometimes venture up to seventy-five feet away from water to feed. They take a wide variety of insects and other invertebrates found in the water, along the stream bed, or on the forest floor.

The tailed frog belongs to what is considered the most primitive of frog families, and you'd have to travel to New Zealand to find its closest relatives. But the uniqueness of the tailed frog makes it well worth the search in the cold, rushing Northwest mountain streams.

Gray Jay

Latin name: *Perisoreus canadensis*

Description: 10 inches; pale gray breast; darker gray wings, tail, nape, and top of head; black bill.

Habitat: Coniferous forests, from 2,000 feet to timberline; also mixed coniferous-deciduous forests.

Naturalists discourage people from feeding wildlife (except at backyard feeders) for several reasons. These can center on either danger to the human (from bites or transfer of disease) or danger to the animal (from a junk food diet or from reliance on a food source that disappears when the tourists do).

But gray jays are not just your ordinary wildlife beggars found hanging around woodland picnic tables. Gray jays are thieves. Bold and smart thieves. This trait is so well known that they are often called "camp-robbers," and their daring exploits are described in several bird books. The long list of audacious acts include grabbing sizzling bacon from a frying pan, entering tents to filch crackers, stealing tobacco and matches, and pecking candles and soap into bits. Camp-robbers are also known to steal bait from traps, follow the sound of gunshots to share in a hunter's kill, and help themselves to freshly caught (and unguarded) fish.

It's tempting to say these birds are sticky-fingered, but they're actually sticky-mouthed. A gray jay has very large salivary glands that exude a sticky mucus, allowing it to extract seeds and insects from crevices with a sticky tongue. This adaptation also allows it to store food for the coming winter. Using its saliva, a gray jay rolls seeds or other food particles into a small rounded lump called a bolus and then attaches it to a twig or conifer needle. By retrieving its caches (at least those not raided by the Steller's jay, a close relative), the gray jay survives the winter without the need to migrate.

These year-round residents are well suited to snow. Gray jays are so nonchalant about freezing temperatures that they begin nesting in March, even if still surrounded by several feet of the white stuff. As might be expected, their nests are particularly well insulated. Often located on a tree limb near the trunk, the nest is a bulky affair made of twigs, bark strips, mosses, and grasses, with a lining of feathers, fur, or grass. The male helps make the nest, but the female alone is responsible for incubating their three to four eggs. After sixteen to eighteen days, the young hatch and both parents feed them. At about fifteen days, the young are ready to leave the nest. Despite their early start, a pair of gray jays raise only one brood per season.

A relative, the Clark's nutcracker (*Nucifraga columbiana*) also breeds while snow is on the ground, and is sometimes also referred to as a camp-robber. But the two gray birds can be easily be told apart because the wings and tail of the nutcracker are black with white markings. Named after explorer William Clark of Lewis and Clark fame, this bird is far less common in Washington and Oregon than the gray jay.

Gray jays are so familiar to people that we've come up with several other names for them, including Canada jay and whiskey-jack (which evolved from an Indian name, *wiskatjan*). But countless hikers, picnickers, and cross-country skiers can attest that the name "camp-robber" is the most fitting.

Glacier Lily

Latin name: *Erythronium grandiflorum*

Description: 6 to 16 inches high; bright yellow recurved six-petaled lily flower, usually one flower per stalk but can be more; two green glossy leaves growing from base of stem.

Habitat: Mountain meadows, stream banks, trailsides, areas of melting snow; from British Columbia to northern Oregon.

Picture this: It's early spring and you're hiking up a mountain trail—but your goal of visiting a meadow in bloom seems as far away as when you began the ascent this morning. Your lungs and your legs are now complaining with every step, and your granola bars and trail mix are long gone. Glancing down at the snow along the path, you're surprised to find a delicate flower, with six upswept butter-yellow petals glowing against the icy whiteness. You stop for a moment to contemplate this. A lily, borne on a slender stalk, melting a hollow as it grows up through inches of snow. The head of the flower droops, as if the glacier lily is looking down at the snow that still surrounds it, pretty impressed with this feat itself. You shift the pack on your back. Well, if this fragile-looking flower can persevere, you can probably manage another mile or so. You set off again, and in a few paces you round a crook in the trail. A sunny southside meadow greets you, filled with thousands of nodding, bobbing, yellow glacier lilies.

You've just experienced two of the glacier lily's endearing qualities: its heartening ability to bloom through the last inches of snow, and the sheer volume of blossoms that can populate one meadow. Later in the season, many different varieties of wildflowers will grow in the same meadow, after these early bloomers have led the way. Although glacier lilies are most numerous at timberline, they can also be found in scattered locations down the mountainside.

A close relative (so close that some guidebooks use the two common names interchangeably) is the avalanche lily, *E. montanum*. Its flowers are white, with a circle of bright yellow at the center. Like glacier lilies, avalanche lilies can grow through melting snow and can reach more than a foot high. Both species have two wavy-edged leaves, each up to eight inches long, at the base of the stem, but the leaves of avalanche lily are typically mottled. The leaves of both species remain long after the flower has died, continuing to photosynthesize and store energy in a bulblike corm underground. This stored energy will be used when the plant flowers the following spring.

Northwest Indian tribes harvested the corms, boiling and eating them or drying them for later consumption. The leaves and flowers are also edible, although, as some wild-foods texts suggest, these flowers are so relatively uncommon that they are best enjoyed by eyes rather than palates. Deer have no such reservations, however, and gobble up the leaves and immature seedpods.

In Canada,

flowers in this genus are known by the common name of "dogtooth violets." "Dogtooth" apparently refers to the shape of the corm, and "violet" is one of those botanically incorrect labels. Across the border here in the United States, some texts call both of these lilies by the name "avalanche," while others prefer "glacier." Most books, like this one, differentiate between the two. This sort of nomenclatural confusion is precisely the reason why plant and animal species are given scientific names. The Latin names are recognized worldwide and ensure that everyone knows which plant or animal is being discussed, regardless of what local name is accepted. The yellow glacier lily is *Erythronium grandiflorum* (its species name means "big-flowered") and the white avalanche lily is *E. montanum* (its species name translates as "of the mountain").

No matter what you choose to call these flowers, they welcome spring and offer a lovely, invigorating greeting to early-season hikers who persevere to reach mountain meadows.

Lightning

Like a minor Zeus, I've thrown around plenty of small lightning bolts. No doubt you have too. Just scuffle across a carpet on a dry day, touch a doorknob, and—*zap*! You've discharged a spark of static electricity. Lightning bolts are a similar discharge of energy on a far grander scale.

The basic principle behind the two releases of electricity are the same. As you walk across the floor, electrons (the negative particles of atoms) are transferred from the carpet to your body. You are now negatively charged, and those electrons will leap from you as you touch something with an attractive positive charge, such as a metal doorknob.

Lightning occurs through the same process, when the lower portion of a thundercloud becomes negatively charged (though scientists are still debating just why and how this occurs). The discharging bolts of lightning, attracted to areas with a positive charge, may flash inside a cloud or between clouds, may shoot sideways from a cloud into the clear sky, or may reach from the sky to the earth. At least we think of a lightning strike as a single bright stroke from the cloud to the ground, but scientists have shown that what occurs is a more complicated process.

As the negatively charged cloud travels, it affects objects directly beneath it, including the ground itself. Positive charges within the objects are powerfully attracted, and this energy rises toward the cloud. When the attraction between the opposite charges is strong enough to overcome the natural resistance of the air, electrons begin to flow from the cloud in what is called a "stepped leader." This invisible or barely luminescent energy flows down in a zigzag pattern (the zigs and zags are the steps of the stepped leader). As the leader nears the ground, positively charged flows of energy soar up meet it, streaming from every object in the immediate area—the streamers of tall objects naturally shoot the highest. Although the streamers can't be seen, a person standing within the affected area might experience this surge within his or her body as a tingling or a rising of hair. As soon as one of the streamers meets the leader, electricity is born.

The powerful electric current flashes *upward* into the cloud at about sixty thousand miles per second, retracing the path of the stepped leader. This upward surge is called the "return stroke," and its brilliant light produces most of the light we see during a strike. A succession of additional electron streams, called "dart leaders," may travel back down the same path, each to be answered with another return stroke. Most strikes have three or four return strokes, occurring in less than half a second, which we perceive as flickering light.

A single lightning bolt may carry one hundred and twenty-five million volts and be as hot as fifty thousand degrees Fahrenheit, five times the temperature of the surface of the sun. The superheating of the air surrounding the bolt causes thunder. The heated air expands rapidly, producing a shock wave. The more powerful the bolt, the louder and deeper in pitch is the resulting thunder.

Because light travels so much faster than sound, we can see distant lightning before hearing its accompanying clap of thunder. You can use this gap to estimate how far away the storm is and whether it's coming in your direction. As soon you see lightning flash, begin counting by seconds (saying "one-one thousand, two-one thousand" or "one-Mississippi, two-Mississippi" helps toward accuracy). Stop counting when you hear the thunder, and divide the number you stopped on by five (sound travels about one mile in five seconds). If you heard the rumble after five seconds, the storm is one mile away; after ten seconds, it is two miles away. By doing this several times, you can tell whether the storm is approaching or receding.

If a lightning storm is headed your way while you're in the mountains, you should consider your location. If you're above timberline, then *you* are likely to be the tallest object around. Move off any exposed ridge or peak as quickly as possible. Do not stand under an isolated tree, or in an open meadow, and stay away from lakes and rivers.

We may think of lightning as a destructive force, but it is also a creative one. The heat from lightning causes nitrogen and oxygen in the air to combine. The resulting nitrogen compounds, brought to the ground by rain, fertilize the soil. Lightning also forms ozone from oxygen. It rises into the upper atmosphere, where it helps protect the earth from ultraviolet light. And watched from a safe location, lightning and thunder create an awe-inspiring, ear-pounding, roof-rattling light show.

Rain, Rain Shadows, and Rain forests

Many people outside the Northwest think "Oregon" and "Washington" are synonyms for "unending rain." Those who live here are well aware that we get most of our rain in the cooler months and usually have rather dry summers and, further, that the seasonal wetness covers only one-third of both states; the largest sections of both Oregon and Washington are on "the dry side," east of the Cascade Mountains.

But *why* do we receive most of our rain from November through March? Why not the other way around? And why does the *west* side get inundated? Why not the other way around?

The answers begin with the Pacific Ocean and end in the mountains. That massive body of water gains and releases heat slowly, maintaining a remarkably even temperature. The water's surface off the Northwest coast has a nearly constant year-round temperature of about fifty degrees Fahrenheit, varying less than five degrees annually. Because the prevailing winds in the Northwest come from the west (shifting between WSW in winter and SW in spring and fall), they travel across that wide, wide ocean to reach us.

The amount of water vapor the air can hold is determined by the temperature of the air; warmer air can carry more moisture than colder air. Winds of about fifty degrees Fahrenheit soak up moisture like a sponge as they blow across the ocean. What happens when the soggy air meets the land depends on the temperature of the land. During winter, the land is colder than the air temperature over the ocean. As the air traveling inland cools, it can't hold as much moisture, so it releases it in the form of fog or rain. During summer, the land is warmer than the air temperature over the ocean, and the incoming air is able to retain its water vapor.

Now throw the Cascades into the mix. As the winds continue to blow across the land, they run smack-dab into the high mountains and are forced to take a detour upward. As the air rises, it cools. As it cools, it dumps moisture in the form of rain or snow, and naturally the western side receives the brunt of this. As the air descends on the eastern side of the Cascades, it again warms up and is now able to reabsorb moisture. The winds again act as a sponge, but this time drawing up water vapor and drying out the land east of the Cascades. Thus the mountain barrier creates the poetically named "rain shadow" on the eastern side.

The Coast Ranges and the Olympic Mountains also wipe up some of that water vapor as the winds are on their way toward the Cascades. The seven-thousand-foot-high Olympics exert a strong influence in the distribution of precipitation. The Queets, Quinault, and especially Hoh River valleys are inundated with an average of more than one hundred and forty inches of rain annually. As a result, the forests of these valleys have earned the name of temperate rain forests. In addition to having the highest rainfall rate found in the contiguous United States, the rain forests are noted for their fog, high humidity, thick comforters of mosses and lichens, and record-size Sitka spruce, western hemlock, Douglas-fir, and western red-cedar.

Meanwhile, the Olympics create a rain shadow so dramatic that pilots call it "the hole in the sky." The dry corridor located on the northeastern, downward side of the range includes the town of Sequim, which annually averages only sixteen inches of rain.

The Northwest's rain, with its resulting rain shadows and rain forests, is birthed by the Pacific Ocean. Considering the ocean's overwhelming influence on the Northwest, it's appropriate that our home is known as the *Pacific* Northwest.

White~Tailed Ptarmigan

Latin name: *Lagopus leucurus*

Description: To 10 inches; plumage white in winter; mottled brown above, with white underparts, in summer; patchy in spring and fall.

Habitat: Alpine and subalpine zone of the Washington Cascades.

Throughout its whole life, the white-tailed ptarmigan tries to look like something else—something inedible. These birds rely heavily on their ability to blend into the background, becoming part of a crisp snowbank in winter or just another boulder in the talus in summer. Females, in particular, are known to sit silently and nearly invisible on their nests as people unwittingly approach. If you do happen to spot a hen, you might be able to touch her or even pick her up before she'd move—but don't. What we might interpret as an attitude of nonchalance or trust would be an extremely stressful experience for the bird.

The ptarmigan achieves its appropriate seasonal camouflage when its feathers molt. As the days begin to lengthen, winter's basic white plumage gives way to mottled darker feathers. The molt begins at the head and progresses down the body, nicely matching the melting snow and emerging turf. From the time the molt begins, the birds avoid pure white expanses of snow. True to their name, they always retain an edge of white feathers on their tails, as well as on their bellies and legs.

As the birds enter their breeding season, the males' one bit of blazing, attention-grabbing coloration becomes more evident as the red combs above their eyebrows inflate. Females also have these combs, but they are so small as to be inconspicuous. A courting male further impresses the female with screaming cries and a strut that alternates between slow and fast.

The won-over female makes her nest in a shallow depression, sometimes under a sheltering bush but often right out in the open. She softens the scrape with dried grasses, lichens, and feathers. Like many birds, she plucks these feathers from her breast, forming a bare spot called a brood patch, which will more readily transfer heat to her eggs than would her insulating feathers. She lays four to eight eggs, leaving them covered with vegetation until the clutch is complete. The male tends to stay with the female and defend the area around the nest, but usually deserts while she is incubating.

The newly hatched chicks are cryptically colored and, like most ground-nesting birds, they develop quickly. Just ten days after hatching they can manage enough lift to get off the ground, and at ten weeks old they have their full flight feathers. The young eat both vegetation and insects; as they grow into adults they will especially favor the buds, leaves, and flowers of dwarf willow.

As winter returns, the birds form flocks divided by gender, or a bird may remain solitary. Along with their snowy winter plumage, ptarmigans

develop dense feathers on both the tops and bottoms of their feet, and their claws compensate for this extra coverage by growing significantly longer. The feathers probably insulate the feet, and the increased surface area acts like a snowshoe; the ptarmigan's fine-feathered feet keep it afloat on deep snows. Sometimes, however, the bird purposefully burrows beneath the powder to reach buried willow buds or as a way to avoid harsh or windy weather.

In reference to their adaptations to snow and their relation to grouse, these birds are sometimes called "snow grouse." If you choose to call them ptarmigans, be sure to leave off the silent "p" when you ptalk about pthem.

Bluebirds

Latin names: *Sialia currucoides* (mountain bluebird); *S. mexicana* (western bluebird)

Description: To 6 inches, depending on species.
Mountain bluebird: males vivid blue with paler bellies;
females gray-brown with some blue markings.
Western bluebird: males have blue back, rusty red breast,
white belly; females are duller.

Habitat: Alpine to lowlands, depending on species.

Since the bluebird is native only to North America, it is not the "bluebird of happiness" that Belgium-born Maurice Maeterlinck had in mind. Instead, his 1909 play, *L'Oiseau bleu,* featured a turtledove that magically turned blue. But Americans quickly associated the phrase with their bright backyard bird that was nearly as common as a robin. The northern arrival of the migrating bluebird was already considered a cheerful announcement that spring was on the way.

Today North America's bluebirds are so scarce that you can be happy if you manage to see one at all. The cause of their decline? Round up the usual suspects: loss of habitat, impact of pesticides, and competition from introduced species. By the 1950s, bluebirds were in serious trouble. The cavity-nesters had relatively few places to lay their eggs as manicured landscaping replaced dead trees and metal fence posts replaced wooden ones. The suitable places that were available were often usurped by introduced species such as the European starling and the house (or English) sparrow. If those bluebirds that did find housing happened to eat insects poisoned with pesticides, their eggs were sometimes too thin-shelled to protect the developing chicks.

Although the most-offensive pesticides have since been banned, the birds are still poisoned (and may die) from eating sprayed insects. And the clearing of forest and suitable bluebird habitat has continued. For decades, individuals and organizations such as the North American Bluebird Society have been helping the beleaguered birds. People play a direct role in increasing bluebird populations by providing them with specially designed nesting boxes. Bluebirds are secondary cavity nesters, which means that they cannot make their own nesting sites but depend on the abandoned tree holes made by flickers and other birds. Their willingness to accept a nesting box as a nursery, and the willingness of concerned people to put up those boxes and maintain them, directly affect the number of bluebirds that hatch each year.

Two of North America's three bluebird species, the western and the mountain, are found in the Cascade Mountains. (The eastern bluebird is found east of the Great Plains.) The mountain bluebird, which spends its summers in the alpine and subalpine zones and prefers the dry eastern side of the Cascades, has fared better than the western because it has suffered less habitat destruction. The western bluebird favors lower elevations on either side of the Cascades. Both species greatly benefit from nest boxes.

During mating season, male bluebirds return to the area where they were born to claim a territory. Their female siblings have no fidelity to the old nest site and have dispersed, which lessens the chance of inbreeding. Once the male has found a suitable area (preferably with more than one nest site—the female will choose which one they will use), he proclaims his territory from a prominent perch. When an intrigued female stops by, he attempts to convince her of the worthiness of his choice by hovering near a nesthole, or by entering it and making eye contact as he pokes his head out. If she is interested enough to have a look inside herself, he may reward her with an insect snack—a token of his ability to be a good provider. After she has been convinced of both the home's and its host's suitability, the two will mate. As with most birds, the male mounts the female, and both move their tails aside to briefly press together their cloacas (the cloaca is the anal opening through which both reproductive and excretory systems discharge). The male's sperm is transferred to the female with this "cloacal kiss."

The female makes a tidy cup-shaped nest from dried grass or tree needles, in which she lays her four to six eggs. Bluebirds may have two broods a year, and the first fledglings may remain in the area to help raise their siblings. A young male from the previous year's brood might even help care for his parent's new offspring if, when he returns to the nest site, he finds his parents have already reclaimed it.

If you are interested in helping to raise more bluebirds, several regional bluebird organizations can use your help. To find the group nearest you, try an Internet computer search, or contact your local National Audubon Society office, or the North American Bluebird Society at P.O. Box 74, Darlington, WI 53530, or www.nabluebirdsociety.org.

Snowshoe Hare

Latin name: *Lepus americanus*

Description: To 16 inches tall; large hind feet; in summer, fur can be various shades of brown; in winter, individuals at high elevations have white fur with black tips on ears.

Habitat: Brushy cover within forests and along streamsides.

onsider the snowshoe hare as a player in a game of skill (or perhaps chance) called Predator vs. Prey. In winter, when many other small mammals are asleep or hidden beneath the snow, the hare remains in the game. This paucity of lower-food-web pawns makes the hare disproportionately the target of powerful predators such as bobcats, foxes, great horned owls, long-tailed weasels, golden eagles, coyotes, mink, goshawks, and lynxes (although the last are rare in the Northwest). Nevertheless, the game is not over quickly. Following the rules of natural selection, the hare gains certain seasonal advantages.

Camouflage, for example. In summer, the snowshoe hare's coat is brownish and blends in with surrounding vegetation. In winter, the hare sports a thicker, warmer coat that is color-coordinated with the snow. The gradual molt in and out of a white coat is not correlated with snowfall, however; it is triggered by the decrease or increase in daylight. Usually this results in the hare sporting a patchy coat against patches of snow, but sometimes the animal becomes quite conspicuous if the snow comes later (or melts earlier in spring) than usual. This seasonal color change earned the animal its other common name, varying hare.

Of course there's no advantage in varying if the hare lives at lower elevations where it rarely snows. These populations simply don't turn white;

they are brown year-round. You'd expect that snowshoe hares claim territory up to timberline, but it's more surprising to learn that they also range to nearly sea level.

Regardless of where it lives or what color its fur is, when a snowshoe hare is out in the open, its greatest defense is simply sitting still and attempting to blend in with the surroundings. If that tactic doesn't work and the chase is on, the fleeing hare zigs and zags, hits speeds of thirty miles per hour and makes bounds up to twelve feet long. The hare's large, furry hind feet allow it to run on top of soft snow and can give it an advantage over a heavier pursuer.

A heavy snow load and those oversized clown-shoe feet also allow it to stand on the snow and reach higher up on bushes and trees to nibble its winter fare of bark, needles, and buds. In the warmer months, it eats grasses, berries, fruit, and many kinds of plants. Like pikas and many rabbits, snowshoe hares have two types of scat (feces). One is hard, dry waste material. The other, soft and green, consists of vegetation that has not been fully digested, and this the hare eats, usually while at rest during the day. This second passage of food through the animal's digestive system allows for absorption of vitamins and other important nutrients. It also allows the animal to eat quickly while in the open and digest more slowly once safely hidden.

If this behavior seems unsavory to humans, the hare's courtship procedure may be even more so. In what has politely been called "unusual" pre-mating behavior, a male and female take turns leaping over one another while urinating on the one below. Foot stomping (also an alarm signal) may precede this.

The outcome is usually four or five babies, called leverets, which are born after a gestation that lasts up to forty days. The female builds no nest but simply births her young in a secluded place. Within hours the fully furred leverets are able to run. They spend their first day or so huddled near their mother, but after this the young scatter, reuniting with their mother only for a brief nursing session at night. Immediately after a litter is born, the female is ready to mate again. She may produce up to three litters a season. (The cyclic population explosions and drops that are notorious in more northern areas do not seem to occur in the Pacific Northwest).

This prodigious output of offspring is another evolutionary tactic that allows the snowshoe hare species to survive the concentrated pressure of wintertime predators. Alertness, concealment, camouflage, and speed also help to even the score. All are important survival techniques of the wary, harried varying hare.

Selected References

Arno, Stephen F. *Northwest Trees*. Seattle: The Mountaineers, 1977.

Corkran, Charlotte C., and Chris Thoms. *Amphibians of Oregon, Washington, and British Columbia: A Field Identification Guide*. Edmonton, Alberta: Lone Pine Publishing, 1996.

Davis, James Luther. *Seasonal Guide to the Natural Year: A Month by Month Guide to Natural Events*. Golden, Colorado: Fulcrum Publishing, 1996.

Ehrlich, Paul R., et al. *The Birder's Handbook: A Field Guide to the Natural History of North American Birds*. New York: Simon & Schuster Inc., 1988.

Evans, Arthur V., and Charles L. Bellamy. *An Inordinate Fondness for Beetles*. New York: Henry Holt and Company, Inc., 1996.

Furtman, Michael. *Black Bear Country*. Minnetonka, Minnesota: NorthWord Press, 1998.

Geist, Valerius. *Elk Country*. Minocqua, Wisconsin: NorthWord Press, Inc., 1991.

Grambo, Rebecca L. *Mountain Lion*. San Francisco: Chronicle Books, 1999.

Grescoe, Audrey. *Giants: The Colossal Trees of Pacific North America*. Boulder, Colorado: Roberts Rinehart Publishers, 1997.

Guard, Jennifer B. *Wetland Plants of Oregon and Washington*. Redmond, Washington: Lone Pine Publishing, 1995.

Gunther, Erna. *Ethnobotany of Western Washington*. Seattle and London: University of Washington Press, 1973.

Harrington, H. D. *Western Edible Wild Plants*. Albuquerque: University of New Mexico Press, 1977.

Harris, Stephen L. *Fire & Ice: The Cascades Volcanoes*. Seattle: The Mountaineers and Pacific Search Press, 1980.

Haskin, Leslie L. *Wild Flowers of the Pacific Coast*. Portland, Oregon: Binfords & Mort, 1967.

Kirk, Ruth, ed. *The Enduring Forests: Northern California, Oregon, Washington, British Columbia, and Southeast Alaska*. Seattle: The Mountaineers, 1996.

Kobalenko, Jerry. *Forest Cats of North America: Cougars, Bobcats, Lynx*. Buffalo, New York: Firefly Books, Inc., 1997.

Kozloff, Eugene N. *Plants and Animals of the Pacific Northwest*. Seattle and London: University of Washington Press, 1978.

Lawrence, Gale. *The Beginning Naturalist: Weekly Encounters with the Natural World*. Shelburne, Vermont: The New England Press, 1979.

Mathews, Daniel. *Cascade-Olympic Natural History: A Trailside Reference*. Portland, Oregon: Raven Editions, 1999.

Maser, Chris. *Mammals of the Pacific Northwest: From the Coast to the High Cascades.* Corvallis: Oregon State University Press, 1998.

Maser, Chris, et al. *The Seen and Unseen World of the Fallen Tree.* General Technical Report PNW-164. Washington, D.C.: Forest Service/Bureau of Land Management, 1984.

Milne, Lorus, and Margery Milne. *National Audubon Society Field Guide to North American Insects and Spiders.* New York: Alfred A. Knopf, Inc., 1980.

Peattie, Donald Culross. *A Natural History of Western Trees.* Cambridge, Massachusetts: The Riverside Press, 1953.

Pyle, Robert Michael. *National Audubon Society Field Guide to North American Butterflies.* New York: Chanticleer Press, Inc., 1997.

Renner, Jeff. *Northwest Mountain Weather: Understanding and Forecasting for the Backcountry User.* Seattle: The Mountaineers, 1992.

Rue, Leonard Lee, and William Owen. *Meet the Beaver.* New York: Dodd, Mead & Co., 1986.

Schaechter, Elio. *In the Company of Mushrooms: A Biologist's Tale.* Cambridge: Harvard University Press, 1997.

Stokes, Donald W. *A Guide to Observing Insect Lives.* Boston: Little, Brown and Co., 1983.

Stokes, Donald W., and Lillian Q. Stokes. *A Guide to Animal Tracking and Behavior.* Boston: Little, Brown and Co., 1983.

———. *A Guide to Bird Behavior, Volume III.* Boston: Little, Brown and Co., 1989.

Storm, Robert M., and William P. Leonard, eds. *Reptiles of Washington and Oregon.* Seattle: Seattle Audubon Society, 1995.

Terres, John K. *The Audubon Society Encyclopedia of North American Birds.* New York: Alfred A. Knopf, Inc., 1987.

Tyler, Hamilton A. *The Swallowtail Butterflies of North America.* Healdsburg, California: Naturegraph Publishers, 1975.

Wexler, Jerome. *From Spore to Spore: Ferns and How They Grow.* New York: Dodd, Mead & Company, 1985.

Williams, Jack. *The Weather Book: An Easy-to-Understand Guide to the USA's Weather.* New York: Vintage Books, 1992.

Index

A-B

C-D

Wanna Get Really Wild?

MORE Uncommon Field Guides
by Patricia K. Lichen
Illustrations by Linda M. Feltner

Backyards

Passionate Slugs & Hollywood Frogs
An Uncommon Field Guide to Northwest Backyards

Hummingbirds flying upside down. Slugs mating while suspended in midair. A muscular mole turning somersaults in its tunnel. So much is happening, minute by minute, in your own backyard. Dip into this *Uncommon Field Guide* to learn the wild secrets happening right outside your door.

Coast & Wetlands

Brittle Stars & Mudbugs
An Uncommon Field Guide to Northwest Shorelines & Wetlands

Body-surfing otters. Racing razor clams. Water-striding insects. Edible cattails. Let this *Uncommon Field Guide* escort you along the fascinating beaches, rocky shorelines, estuaries, rivers, and marshlands of the Pacific Northwest.